*Literary
Romanticism
in
America*

Literary
Romanticism
in
America

Edited by WILLIAM L. ANDREWS

LOUISIANA STATE UNIVERSITY PRESS

BATON ROUGE AND LONDON

Copyright © 1981 by Louisiana State University Press

Manufactured in the United States of America

Designer: Albert Crochet
Typeface: Linotype Sabon
Typesetter: G&S Typesetters
Printer and binder: Thomson-Shore, Inc.

LIBRARY OF CONGRESS CATALOGING IN PUBLICATION DATA

Main entry under title:

Literary romanticism in America.

1.   American literature—History and criticism—
Addresses, essays, lectures. 2. Romanticism—United
States—Addresses, essays, lectures. I. Andrews,
William L., 1946–
IS169.R6L5   810'.9'145   80-24365
ISBN 0-8071-0760-3

The editor gratefully acknowledges permission to reprint portions of the
material herein, which have appeared in somewhat different form as the fol-
lowing: John Seelye, "The Measure of His Company: Richard M. Nixon in
Amber," *Virginia Quarterly Review*, LIII (Autumn, 1977); the section on
Mather's life of Sir William Phips, in Seelye, *Prophetic Waters: The River in
American Life and Literature* (Oxford University Press, 1977); Louis D.
Rubin, Jr., "Thomas Wolfe and the Place He Came From," *Virginia Quarterly
Review*, LII (Spring, 1976).

To Lewis Leary—teacher,
scholar, and friend

Contents

Preface

"The essence of romanticism," observes Robert E. Spiller in *The Cycle of American Literature*, "is the ability to wonder and to reflect." This essentially American, as well as romantic, imaginative and intellectual attitude toward the world has been for better or worse the birthright of the American writer from the founding of this country forward. Tracing the fate of this birthright, whether treasured, rejected, compromised, or sold by writers or schools of writers, constitutes one of the most important tasks of literary historians and critics as they seek to define the Americanness of American literature. The essays collected here propose a number of original conclusions about the uses to which such writers as Franklin, Emerson, Hawthorne, Frederick Douglass, Thomas Wolfe, Allen Tate, and Walker Percy put their wondering and reflecting faculties. At the same time the essays point a direction in which the American writer's romantic birthright has developed, suggesting in the process how this development has affected the evolution of a peculiarly American tradition in literature.

The book opens where it must, with Ralph Waldo Emerson, the first major articulator and exponent of the American romantic perspective on man and society. After arguing that the distinctiveness of America in the world's eyes lies in this country's "experiment in democracy," Clarence Gohdes sets out to show how the principles of Emersonian romantic idealism undergird the American faith in government of, by, and for the people. Demonstrating the presence of this link between America's romantic intellectual tradition and its democratic political tradition has far-reaching ramifications, as subsequent essays in the collection attest. Gohdes' essay not only introduces the reader to Emerson as America's democrat-idealist par excellence; it also posits a key theme for the rest of the book—how the American writer's response to his romantic cultural inheritance becomes almost inevitably a social, if not a political, act.

While Gohdes points out how romantic idealism served as a moral and political guide for an individualistic Emerson at odds with public opinion or governmental policy, Arlin Turner plays turnabout with the example of Nathaniel Hawthorne. When popular prejudice found an ally in facile idealism, and romanticizing national history became a ready way of dismissing its complexities, Hawthorne, in Turner's view, took pains to disavow what had been adulterated in his American writer's birthright. In the name of intellectual independence, Hawthorne found it necessary to stand aloof from the same brand of romantic idealism that sustained the rugged intellectual individualism of Emerson. The usefulness of this aloofness to Hawthorne when he wrote as "questioning observer and interpreter of America" is amply documented in Turner's study. Turner shows that the habit of detachment and objectivity vis-à-vis the subjects of his romances stood Hawthorne in good stead when he decided to address the social scene in America past or present. No less than the romance writer did Hawthorne the social commentator write with acuteness and judiciousness, for in social, as well as moral or psychological, contexts he felt characteristically obliged to render both the light and the dark of his subject. Thus from fictionalized historian of the Puritan era to contemporary pundit on Victorian America, Hawthorne emerges from Turner's essay a romanticist more disposed to reflect than to wonder, to discover in the nation's past the seeds of mounting irrepressible conflicts, not a glorious manifest destiny.

As social and intellectual conflicts at mid-century centered more and more around the fate of black people in America, a group of Afro-American writers emerged in the 1850s with their own contribution to the romantic tradition in American literature. Out of the fugitive-slave narrative, an often collaborative effort between ex-slaves and abolitionist amanuenses, came a small group of novels and autobiographies that established an independent prose narrative tradition in Afro-American letters. The interrelated purposes and import of these books, in the opinion of William L. Andrews, united them and their authors into the first Afro-American literary renaissance, a counterpart of the much more celebrated American renaissance of the 1850s. Led by Frederick Douglass in the autobiography and Martin R. Delany in the novel, this largely unnoticed black literary movement was characterized by the sort of imaginative idealism, intellectual individualism, and humanitarian concern that distinguished most romantic writing of the nineteenth century. In addition, such perennial themes in American romantic writing as rebellion, alienation, and the quest for selfhood appeared in a penetrating new light when the early black writer focused his perspective on them. With these themes foremost, "The 1850s: The First Afro-American Literary Renaissance" documents a seminal though as yet largely unread chapter in black American literary history. The evidence of intellectual and imaginative kinship between the two renaissances in American letters during the 1850s suggests that the often discretely categorized *mainstream* and *minority* literary traditions share a common romantic heritage in the nineteenth century.

With Louis D. Rubin's essay, the focus of attention shifts to three writers of the modern South and the applicability of romantic literary modes to their purposes. Professor Rubin discusses "Thomas Wolfe and the Place He Came From" in order to affirm that Wolfe's relationship to the South was similar to that of most writers of the Southern Renascence, even though his manner of expressing that relationship was not. Although Eugene Gant appears only to despise the land of his youth instead of maintaining the classic love-hate ambivalence toward it typified in Faulkner's Quentin Compson, Rubin believes that Eugene's lingering feeling for the "South that burned like Dark Helen in [his] blood" betrays a "passionate emotional attachment" to the Piedmont South that was true of Gant's creator also. As a result of this attachment and moral involvement, Wolfe wrote with an immediacy, subjectivity, and self-consciousness that have often been judged the very antithesis of the traditional southern literary temper. While Rubin considers this brand of romanticism in Wolfe's writing to be distinctive, he thinks it by no means unprecedented in the history of southern literature. His identification of a tradition of southern writing based on a "passionate and direct assertion of personality" illuminates yet another obscure vein of romantic expression in American letters. Likewise, his reminder that Wolfe, like his more classical southern literary forebears, took the American self grounded in the South and traced its attempts to realize the American Dream, provides a unifying framework in which to view such southern literary contrasts to Wolfe as Allen Tate and Walker Percy.

The autobiographical fictional mode pioneered by Wolfe in modern southern literature is also exemplified in Allen Tate's novel *The Fathers* (1938), discussed in C. Hugh Holman's essay "*The Fathers* and the Historical Imagination." However, Holman is interested in Tate as an American writer who borrowed from the English romantic tradition, in this case from the historical novel of Walter Scott, to create a literary form suitable to American experience and cultural needs. To Holman, *The Fathers* belongs to the traditional "historical imagination" of the South, typified by Ellen Glasgow's novels, in its investigation of conflicting social codes, values, and ideals in the South through the prism of the Civil War. But the novel belongs also to a larger national *Bildungsroman* tradition, because its hero is not the passive protagonist of historical fiction in the Scott mold, but a "spectator-narrator" whose understanding of the world and his own experience in it emerges as he tells his story retrospectively. Such experimentation with retrospective narrative invites comparison with *Moby-Dick*, *The Blithedale Romance*, *My Ántonia*, and *The Great Gatsby*. It also endows *The Fathers* with a density of symbolic implication and a Jamesian or Fordian structure that urge a more complete consideration of what the possibilities of the historical imagination are and how they may be applied. By showing the reader how the historical romanticist has moved beyond merely recreating the past to dramatizing the process by which the past is interpreted, Holman points out one direction that the reflective mode of the romantic imagination has pursued since the nineteenth century.

The fate of that other romantic faculty, wonder, in the work of the contemporary southern novelist Walker Percy is the subject of Panthea Reid Broughton's "Walker Percy and the Innocent Eye." Percy's protagonists all share a preoccupation with reclaiming their vision, Broughton points out, so that they may recover the distance that stands between them and the world around them. Desiring "access to being," liberation from the malaise of isolation and abstraction of the self, they devise various ways to clarify their perceptions and regain the resonance and meaning of their experience. Broughton believes these efforts hark back to the cultivation of naïveté, wonder, and innocence that romantic writers, particularly in America, have engaged in since the early nineteenth century. But while "the innocent eye" worked for Emerson as a precondition of true perception and for Clemens as a penetrating narrative point of view, its redemptive value for the alienated twentieth-century American is severely questioned in Percy's novels. Like Hawthorne, whose protagonists often suffer from spiritual maladies similar to those that plague Percy's heroes, Walker Percy distrusts the substitution of seeing for being as a strategem of life. After attaining their special insights and visionary perspectives on themselves and their fellows, the observer figures in both writers' work realize they are no closer to a lasting felt sense of life. Visionary perception alone proves an insufficient conduit for human feeling and spiritual interconnection. What this conclusion in Percy's work (as well as in Hawthorne's) signifies is that America's romantic tradition is not as naïve as its pronouncements about the necessity of naïveté in art suggest. As Turner, Andrews, and Broughton show, American romanticism has endured at least partly because it has embraced as checks and balances both wonder *and* reflection, intuition *and* skepticism, transcendent individualism *and* democratic brotherhood.

In the concluding essay of this collection, John Seelye looks at the evolution of that supreme American romance—the rise of the self-made man—in classic biographical and autobiographical narratives of the eighteenth and nineteenth centuries. In the hands of Cotton Mather, Benjamin Franklin, Frederick Douglass, and Horatio Alger, the American success hero assumed the habiliments of a cultural ideal, while the story of how he "made it" became formularized into popular myth. What Seelye is interested in is the disjunctiveness of this myth of success in the work of the authors he selects; he finds a thematic schism separating "the fiction of the self-made man" and the "truth of the clay foot of the climber." How that schism gets embroidered over through art, artifice, and sometimes sheer chutzpah is Seelye's chief concern as analyst of Mather's biography of Sir William Phips (1702), Franklin's *Autobiography* (1791), Douglass' *Narrative* (1845), and Alger's popular novels of the 1860s and 1870s. From the analysis of these books against their sociopolitical background comes a sobering insight into the complex of egoistic, economic, and political factors that have shaped the classic American success story into the near-fantastic forms it has often taken. The title character of the essay, Richard M. Nixon, is offered as proof of the barnaclelike tenacity with which the success myth and its hero, no matter how suspect or discredited they may have become, still cling to America's consciousness. So long as life imitates art, Seelye's essay implies, America's men on the make will package themselves according to the images selected and promoted by today's Mathers, Franklins, and Algers, who with poll as well as pen have shown themselves mightier than the sword. In the face of this continuing devaluation by inflation of the American culture hero, Americans will do well to adopt the pragmatic, not the innocent, eye in front of the television, reserving their wonder and reflection for what it takes no romantic vision to see is the "nothing that is not there and the nothing that is."

Literary
Romanticism
in
America

An
American Author
as Democrat

❧

CLARENCE GOHDES

During World War II one of my friends, an anthropologist by profession, served as an officer of our State Department, advising on the essential or nonessential nature of shipments to be made to the west coast of South America. In going over the invoices submitted for his inspection he noticed that there were orders for a surprising amount of florida water, a kind of toilet water, to be shipped from a particular firm in New York City. Certainly, he thought, florida water could be regarded as nonessential with cargo space at a premium. But he noticed that his statements to that effect were completely disregarded by his superiors, who had dwelt long in the area; and the orders went through. When an opportunity for a vacation came along, he indulged himself in anthropological pursuits in a rural and very backward community. The florida water question still bothered him, but upon inquiry he soon found out that the local witch doctors—in plentiful supply—used that particular brand of florida water as an important element in their ceremonies. The victim of a spell or of a demon causing a disease had to be sprinkled with the contents of one of those bottles from New York. No other variety, he was assured, was "strong enough." So far as the natives of that section of Latin America were concerned, the witches at least considered the United States of America a vitally important source of florida water—and very little more.

If one asks in a more general way, What has our country stood for in the eyes of foreign nations? no neat answer readily emerges, for the attitude of the world toward any of its constituent nations varies from time to time and is subject to sudden gusts of

1

emotion. Economics, politics, and even witchcraft, it seems, may condition the reaction. The materials for an answer to such a question abound in the books and articles written by travelers who may have visited our shores for six weeks or six months, who may have seen New York but not Chicago, who may have come with an open mind or with a fixed determination to be displeased. One may illustrate the difficulties best by setting forth some of the aspects of our country and of our people which have from time to time been noted in books of travel.

A hundred years ago we seemed to foreigners, like Charles Dickens, to be especially devoted to the habit of tobacco chewing. More lately we have shifted to gum. Whether the gum chewing has anything to do with it, foreign observers credit us with having better teeth than most peoples—and our dentists with being the best in the world. Visitors from countries with an established church have viewed us as seething in sectarian confusion and as having produced only two religions of our own: Mormonism and Christian Science. We have always appeared as a very busy people, humming with activity. Theodore Roosevelt's phrase for the idea was "the strenuous life." The absence of a leisured class has impressed one writer after the other. One of them once asked an American friend, "Don't you really have any leisured class at all?" and the answer came back, "O, yes, only we call them *tramps.*" A traveling impresario from Italy once picked out as the four most distinctive American products: apples, oysters, white bread, and women. The last of these usually have come in for comment, for both Europeans and Asiatics readily note the unusual respect paid to ladies in this country and sometimes have expressed astonishment at the freedom with which the sexes commingle. In the 1880s one travel-book writer summed up the woman question as follows: "At Cairo," he said, "a woman is an idealized slave"; in Florence, "a cherished article of domestic chattel"; in New York, "an equal, and more often than not, an aggravating, overbearing confederate." Another Italian was particularly impressed by the lack of iron gratings between women employees and their male customers, and still another from a Catholic country found the maidenly habit of flirting to be very characteristic. Boston, he thought, was most notorious in this respect. And he cited as an example a couple whom he saw seated on the grass in the Public Garden, the girl reading aloud from *Harper's Magazine*, the boy shading her with a parasol. Only one change is needed to make that picture of flirting in Boston perfect—the magazine should have been the *Atlantic Monthly*. There was a time when our sexual morality astonished the European travel-book writer; we seemed to be a whole nation of Darbys and Joans. But very recently even the French have been shocked by our novels and the folkways of our young men, and perhaps the old AEF ditty will eventually be revised to read, "The Americans are a naughty race, *parlez-vous.*"

Our people have long been classed as the leading newspaper and magazine readers, and the size of our papers, daily and Sunday, still is a wonder of the New World, like Niagara Falls or Yellowstone Park. Widespread education at state expense seemed, years ago, to be one of our chief accomplishments, but our colleges were only faintly praised as offering very practical training. In architecture we seemed merely to be imitative, until the skyscrapers at length sprang up to give us distinction. In music, also, we lagged, but more recently our symphony orchestras have begun to exact admiration, and our composers are becoming known; though for several decades our specialty has appeared to be dance music. Even in remote villages in the Near East one can hear American "rock," or at least a version of it. We are also recognized as the chief purveyors of the most popular dramatic entertainment ever known to mankind. Not only the movies, but furs, tobacco, cotton, automobiles, airplanes, and even Parker 51 fountain pens have at one time or another seemed to be our most cherished economic products. The procession of our men of daring has run from the Indian fighter and the cowboy to the Chicago gangster. The mixture of races in our melting pot has always been a lively topic for travelers to comment upon—and of course the American Negro has prompted a whole literature by himself. Earlier in our history we had been again and again charged with not paying our debts! Now we are charged with being Uncle Shylock.

Heinrich Heine once observed that in the beginning God created man in his own image, and ever since man has been striving to return the compliment. Certainly men have created a very human image of their fellowmen.

Such aspects of American life as I have used to illustrate—very human as they are—belong to the realm of the superficial, though I should immediately admit that the superficial is of no little importance in the field of international relations. When one looks for something weightier in answer to the question, What has America stood for in the eyes of the world? there are two chief aspects of the answer.

At the time of the establishment of our government, and for many decades thereafter, the United States represented to the intelligence of the world most fundamentally an experiment in democracy. The advanced liberals looked upon us with favor, drank to the health of George Washington, and prophesied all manner of future accomplishment to come from the experiment. The conservatives, a more powerful set in that they usually controlled their own governments, regarded us with disfavor as a nation of plebeians playing with political dynamite that one day would blow up and perhaps injure Europe with the falling wreckage. Late in the nineteenth century, even social-minded John Ruskin, who described himself as a "peculiar Tory," could not forbear twitting American visitors about their "republican experiment." And Matthew Arnold solemnly expressed the opinion that "few stocks could be trusted to grow up properly without having a priesthood and an aristocracy to act as their schoolmasters." We often lay the blame for traditional, old-fashioned isolationism upon the square shoulders of the American people, but an important factor was undoubtedly the hostile attitude of the conservatives of Europe, who despised democracy as a plague and looked upon our future with foreboding. The great test, of course, came at the time of the Civil War, when the broadest intellectual significance of the question was exactly what Abraham Lincoln stated it to be—a test whether this nation, or any nation so conceived and so dedicated, could long endure. The fact that our government did endure was of enormous consequence in shaping foreign opinion, for the dire prophecies of the conservatives were shown by events to have been as false as yesterday's science. The first really important general answer to the question, What has the world thought of us? is to be found in the fact that we have represented an experiment in democracy.

America has also appeared to the world as an example of phenomenal wealth, and of power based upon that wealth. The riches of our country were, of course, a matter of prophecy from the earliest days of exploration. Indeed, exploration was largely motivated by the dreams of wealth. Years after the establishment of the nation, the chief view of our wealth, I think, was that the common man enjoyed a greater prosperity than his European cousin. It was not until after the Civil War, with the astonishing progress of industry, that we came to be identified with riches in spectacular amount. And our reputation in this regard has developed so amazingly in the present century as to make pale the golden vision of America that seemed so enticing in the last decades of the nineteenth.

So far as power is concerned, probably the first overt demonstration that impressed the intellectual world came in 1898 with our war against Spain, when, with one of those ironies occasionally seen in history, the chief American nation turned against the very mother of American colonization and achieved a quick and emphatic victory. This premonitory sign that here was a new element of considerable importance in reckoning the balance of power was soon followed by two wars which proved beyond question that the United States of America represented might. At the present time, it may be said, our country stands as one of the giants of history, holdings in one hand billions of dollars and in the other weapons of indescribable power—the symbols of what the United States stands for in the eyes of the world. Uncle Sam may very well show a look of bewilderment upon his erstwhile provincial face.

It may be interjected that our claims to recognition as an experiment in democracy have been sadly obscured by the vast shadows cast by wealth and power, even though in times of crisis we ourselves assert them with fervor. Change and experiment elsewhere have come so thick and fast that we are now the oldest among the governments of the chief nations of the earth. The word experiment thus seems outmoded, even though we all trust that we shall never cease to experiment.

Considering, now, the opinion that we have stood longest before the eyes of the intellectual world as an experiment in democracy, the question may be asked of the literary historian, How well do the American authors illustrate the chief claim of America upon the world's intelligence? The answer, again, is not easy to derive, for art is art and political and social philosophy are political and social philosophy—despite the efforts of literary critics during the 1930s to make an olio of the three. How American is American literature? . . . How French is French literature? 'Tis hard to say.

Certainly our literary men of past times, with very few exceptions, have been sturdy believers in the democratic experiment. Their political and social views impressed the critics of nineteenth-century England at least as being "radical," in the older European sense of that word. Even the gentle Longfellow, teacher and translator of Dante, refused a decoration offered by the Italian government on the ground that as a citizen of a republic and as an American it would be improper for him to accept it. But do the actual writings of our major authors reflect much of the idea for which we have stood in the eyes of the world? Poe and Henry James we may as well dismiss as belonging to the no-man's-land of art. Though James dealt frequently in his fiction with Americans suffering at the hands of conspiring or hostile Europeans, he told his brother William that he wished to write in such a way that no one could detect his nationality. That, he said, would be "more civilized." Assuredly we should have no objections to James's view, for all that we can wish for our writers is that they be as American as they *unconsciously* can be. Hawthorne, strong as the instincts of the artist were in him, would never have been willing to pass for anyone but an American. In fact, when certain Englishmen, hearing of the very favorable criticism of *The Scarlet Letter* in England, assumed on that

account that its author could only be British, he was disgusted
instead of flattered.

But what about that author who was capable of elaborating a
plot dealing with a pair of Siamese twins, one of whom was a
Methodist and a teetotaler, the other a freethinker and a devotee
of the bottle? Mark Twain has been read by millions in Germany,
Russia, and elsewhere, who have considered him a veritable mir-
ror of the American character. The British critics of the nineteenth century claimed to have found our most original contribution to the world's store of literature in our humorous writing,
and surely Mark Twain stands at the head of our vast procession
of literary jesters. But, I should say, he has offered to the world
primarily a hearty picture of the cheerful irreverence that has
been one of the accompaniments of our democratic life—an important picture, to be sure, yet not a central one.

When we consider the work of Whitman and of Emerson, I
think we approach a more obvious centrality, for these two men
have perhaps come nearest to expressing directly and indirectly
what John Dewey called "the metaphysical implications of the
idea of democracy." Of the two, Whitman is perhaps more wide-
ly read today at home and abroad, but, considering also the days
gone by, Emerson is the one whose message has been more wide-
ly disseminated. For that reason he is to be preferred as our point
of concentration. However, another reason leads one to choose
Emerson—and that is the fact that from him Whitman drew ideas
and inspiration on a variety of topics, including the metaphysics
of democracy. "Master, these shores *you* have found," wrote
Whitman in a letter addressed to Emerson and printed in the second edition of *Leaves of Grass*. In a more homely metaphor he
remarked, "I was simmering, simmering, simmering. Emerson
brought me to a boil."

We might remind ourselves at this point that Emerson has
been a potent influence upon a number of American writers.
Whitman, Thoreau, Emily Dickinson, Edwin Arlington Robinson
—these and more have felt the tonic effect of his ideas. In Europe
also the list of those who have acknowledged his catalytic stimu-

lus includes the names of Hermann Grimm, Matthew Arnold, George Eliot, Nietzsche, Tyndall, and Huxley. In centering our thoughts upon him, we are, accordingly, not merely gratifying a patriotic antiquarianism in brushing the dust off the notions of an ex-Unitarian clergyman who lectured on village platforms and later made essays of his lectures—a man full of the chill of his native New England. We deal with one of the most influential thinkers who ever raised his voice in America. Indeed, Emerson's ideas have exerted influence in circles where the name of Thomas Jefferson has never been heard.

When one examines the method of Emerson's thinking and his intellectual climate it may seem astounding that he could have wielded so much influence, for he was not a formal philosopher, he could not argue his points, and his sentences stand as single sentries instead of members of a company bent upon concerted attack or defense. Yet those sentences which stand thus alone are of singular brilliance. Some of them we quote as proverbs without knowing who wrote them: To think is to act; Beauty is its own excuse for being; He builded better than he knew; A foolish consistency is the hobgoblin of little minds; Hitch your wagon to a star. But despite the rhetorical coruscations, Emerson's method of writing strikes us as that of a poetic thinker incapable of coherent and close reasoning.

We may be bothered also by the fact that he pulls his shining thoughts out of the old stream of Neoplatonic idealism—and certainly that seems an old-fashioned place to fish. Moreover, he sometimes retires to a particular pool of mysticism just off the Neoplatonic river. He always returns with a creel full of fine specimens, but most of us can't fish in that pool, for there one uses neither tackle nor bait. The fish just come. For some time T. S. Eliot and his school have nodded in the direction of Saint John of the Cross, but to our age the method of the mystic is likely to seem very romantic. Emerson's idealism may well appear like escapism to a generation absorbed as is ours in the exploration of man's environment. Indeed, to many of his contemporaries he seemed far removed from this mundane sphere. A hundred years ago the story was told that one of the prophets of the Millerites learned his lesson from Emerson. The Millerites, let me hasten to add, were a peculiar sect who from time to time have prophesied the definite hour and minute at which the world would end. One of their prophets, so the yarn goes, rushed into the lobby of Boston's Parker House Hotel to sound the alarm. Therein he saw the two chief heretics of New England quietly reading—Theodore Parker and Ralph Waldo Emerson. Striding up to Parker, the Millerite shouted: "Mr. Parker. Mr. Parker. Don't you know that the world will end tonight?" "That doesn't bother me, my good man," replied Parker; "I live in Boston." Proceeding to Emerson, the prophet again sounded his warning, "Tonight the world will end." "Splendid," came the answer; "man can get along much better without it."

The idea of democracy today is assumed to lie in the realm of economics and politics. To a humanist, however, democracy is a humanistic conception. When we turn to the particular aspect of Emerson's beliefs that provided him with his faith in democracy, we come to his idea of man. His fundamental conception is that man shares the divine nature. Man has God within him. "In all my lectures," Emerson wrote, "I have taught one doctrine, namely, the infinitude of the private man." The pendulum had swung far away from the notion of man held by the old Calvinists of New England. Jonathan Edwards had expressed very concretely the total-depravity concept with the dismaying sentence, "Man's heart is a serpent, spitting poison at God." And now Emerson had calmly reacted as far as possible in the opposite direction. "God defend me," he prayed, "from ever looking at a man as an animal." And he jotted these words in his journal: "God manifest in the flesh of every man is a perfect rule of social life. Justify yourself to an infinite Being in the hostler and dandy and stranger, and you shall never repent."

It is impossible to attach Emerson's central doctrine concerning man to any specific source. William Ellery Channing, representing the older Unitarian school from which Emerson emerged, had repeated again and again that timeless phrase, "the dignity of human nature." But divinity is beyond mere dignity. The intense faith in human perfectibility that had grown up in the eighteenth century Emerson, like all men of his age, was heir to. Moreover, the conjunction of man and God was implicit in the faith of the mystics. All that we can safely say, then, in regard to the sources of his supreme faith in man is that the reaction against Calvinism, the romantic doctrines of perfectibility, and the mystic vision—all provided a congenial atmosphere in which such a view could develop.

Belief in the divinity of man is a general idea not at all uncommon in the history of thought, and surely we can claim for Emerson no originality here. What is most original in his doctrine comes in connection with his belief in the source of man's highest knowledge, namely, what he calls the "moral sentiment." Now that term was tossed about in the eighteenth century and in the early nineteenth almost as frequently as the expression "inferiority complex" has been bandied about during the last fifty years. Emerson used the words moral sentiment to describe the voice of moral law within the mind and emotions of man. Sometimes he called it the religious sentiment, but much more frequently the moral sentiment. If man, with God within, of course, could be made to correspond to a biological cell, then the moral sentiment might be considered to be the nucleolus of that cell. The moral sentiment is, for Emerson, the highest source of truth. It is the voice of God, if you like—although God to Emerson was an impersonal Over-Soul. Again and again he refers to this sentiment. In his thinking Emerson has been compared to an expert golfer, and the comparison has a peculiar aptness, for our poetic thinker advances his thought by a series of separate pronouncements, just as the golfer advances the ball with a series of separate strokes. But as a golfer Emerson has, let us say, a tendency to slice the ball. (Perhaps the tendency is due to his Neoplatonic stance.) Whenever the ball is in a very difficult position, he reaches into his bag for an old well-worn club, and with it he invariably lays the ball near the pin. The old club has two words inscribed on it: MORAL SENTIMENT.

Man shares the divine nature, and the highest truths that he can know are the product of his moral sentiment. Here we have the aboriginal basis of Emerson's philosophy of man, the grounds

for his faith in democracy. But there are three subsidiary consid-
erations—three corollaries. And in spite of what I have said about
Emerson's incapacity for cogent argument, it seems to me that
there is a kind of logic in the way that these three corollaries
hang on to the general belief that has been outlined.

In the first place, if man shares the divine nature, there is need
for self-trust. (Emerson, with moral law always supreme in his
mind, insists that self-trust is a *duty*.) Self-trust is necessary, for
in the last analysis it means reliance on God within. "Trust thyself; every heart vibrates to that iron string." That is the motif
of the famous essay "Self-Reliance," and a refrain repeated
throughout his writings from the earliest to the latest. The travel-
book writers often mentioned self-reliance as a characteristic
trait of Americans, and the major European students of the United States, like Alexis de Tocqueville and Viscount James Bryce,
have concurred. Carlo Gardini, one of the ablest of Italian writers
on America (1887), and a seasoned traveler, stated the "one
cardinal principle underlying every American concept" to be
"utmost self-dependence of the individual." So very natural does
the doctrine of self-reliance seem that Emerson's version of it
has been taken by some Americans to be an apologia for natural
self-assertiveness, and even the basis for the predatory tactics be-
loved of sales managers. Americans developed self-reliance because of the necessity of adaptation to a vast frontier requiring
conquest—so goes one of the arguments. But note how, in reality,
Emersonian self-reliance has little to do with outward circumstance; it derives vitality from the fundamental doctrine that man
has God within him.

A second corollary follows upon the doctrine. If man shares
the divine nature, nothing can stand in the way of man's progress.
The untold power of the Over-Soul is tapped, and since with
God all things are possible, so with man. Here is the notorious
Emersonian optimism at its fullest height. It staggers us with its
implications. With seraphic confidence Emerson proclaims: "Let
the single man plant himself indomitably upon his own instincts
and there abide, and the huge world will come round to him."
"Things" may be in the saddle and riding mankind, but man will

never succumb to conditions, for there are two laws not reconciled—law for man and law for thing. And the law for man, since
it is law for God, posits amelioration in society. "There is no
lost good," he says, and over the winter glaciers he sees "the summer glow, and through the wild-piled snowdrift the warm rose-
buds below." "The destiny of organized nature is amelioration,
and who can tell its limits?"

Though he lived into the year 1882, Emerson seems to have
realized already in 1866 that his real work was done. At that
time he appears to have become aware of a constitutional weakness which would cripple his powers—a weakness he attributed
to heredity. As a matter of fact, he was quite justified in his belief
that he would lose his powers, for in his later days he was the
victim of what used to be called "softening of the brain." But his
poem called "Terminus," in which he forecasts his disintegration,
ends with these words:

> As the bird trims her to the gale,
> I trim myself to the storm of time,
> I man the rudder, reef the sail,
> Obey the voice at eve obeyed at prime:
> "Lowly faithful, banish fear,
> Right onward drive unharmed;
> The port, well worth the cruise, is near,
> And every wave is charmed."

It is apparent that the optimistic belief in human progress was
instilled deep in Emerson's nature, and that it was not merely a
concept for abstract speculation.

The third corollary may be stated succinctly: if every man—
Joe Doaks as well as Plato—has God within him, then every man
is of equal importance. When Thomas Carlyle considered the
great men of history, he called them heroes, really supermen,
whom the ordinary mortal should cherish in hero worship. When
Emerson viewed the Napoleons and Goethes and Montaignes of
the world, he called them Representative Men.

In his stress upon the powers and importance of the individual,
Emerson often seems to be almost an anarchist. He was an ad-

vocate of forty-four freedoms, and any threat to the parity of the individual touched the trigger of his dissent. "Leave this hypocritical prating about the masses," he advises. "Masses are rude, lame, unmade, pernicious in their demands and influences, and not to be flattered but to be schooled. I wish not to concede anything to them, but to tame, drill, divide and break them up, and draw individuals out of them. . . . When [government] reaches its true law of action, every man that is born will be hailed as essential." That government alone is good, he maintains, which least thwarts the sacred liberty of the citizen. Hence, the less government the better.

The state is thus subordinate—a means to an end—and may be changed, in fact, must be changed, according to the desire of the members of the state. Even in the trying days just before the Civil War he was bold enough to declare: "At this moment, the terror of old people and of vicious people is lest the Union of these states be destroyed: as if the Union had any other real basis than the good pleasure of a majority of the citizens to be united. But the wise and just man will always feel that he stands on his own feet; that *he* imparts strength to the State, not receives security from it; and that if all went down, he and such as he would quite easily combine in a new and better constitution." In one of his poems he sums up his attitude toward the state by asserting that man should serve the law for man by living for friendship, love, truth, and harmony—and the state must follow "as Olympus follows Jove." And in another connection he prophesies that state alone can survive "in which injury to the least member is recognized as damage to the whole." How far removed are these opinions from the ideologies that have envisaged the state as a Juggernaut under whose wheels the citizen is to be flung whenever a little mud threatens to bog it down!

The groundwork of Emerson's conception of democracy is firmly rooted in idealistic philosophy, not in societal externals. It proceeds from within; it is humanistic. Democracy is founded on faith, not positivistic tenets. It is an ideal that inspires, though is never to be reached in all particulars. That awe-inspiring creature—man—must trust himself, must believe that he is destined to a good end, and must consider his fellows his equals because he has within him a cosmic force of abounding beauty, goodness, and truth—a force most completely revealed to the mind and emotions through the moral sentiment.

So much for the theory. But what about Emerson as a practicing democrat? Did he perform his duties as one of those divine integers who were to make the state? We may illustrate from his biography. He appears to have cast his ballot regularly and when called upon played his part in the affairs of his community and of the nation. Shortly after he was married and settled in Concord, Massachusetts, he was elected hogreeve of his town. That was, to be sure, a humble office, for its duties consisted of preventing straying farm animals from damaging the gardens and the fields of his neighbors. There is, alas, no record of his success in the performance. The town meeting, the local unit in New England government, he attended regularly, but he preferred to remain silent and admire the natural dignity and political sagacity exhibited by the rustics of his neighborhood. He often commented upon their natural eloquence and the picturesqueness of their speech. He represented his townsmen upon public occasions, and the number of speeches and poems he composed for local affairs is large. The best-known example of these is probably the hymn he wrote to be sung to the tune of "Old Hundredth" when a monument was erected in Concord to honor its citizens who had died in one of the first battles of the Revolutionary War. That hymn contains the oft-quoted lines: "Here once the embattled farmers stood, And fired the shot heard round the world."

So far as national affairs are concerned, the only appointment to record is membership on a board of visitors selected by Lincoln in 1863 to inspect West Point. John Burroughs, who was there at the time, has left us a picture of Emerson engaged in his duties. "My attention," he tells us, "was attracted to this eager, alert, inquisitive farmer, as I took him to be. Evidently, I thought, this is a new thing to him; he feels the honor that has been conferred upon him, and he means to do his duty and let no fact or word or thing escape him. When the rest of the Board looked

dull or fatigued or perfunctory, he was all eagerness and attention. . . . I shall never forget his serene, unflinching look."

In voting at the town meetings, in sharing the work of school
or library committees of Concord or in visiting West Point,
Emerson was what we should call a good citizen. But more important than the faithful performance of duty was his outspoken
criticism of the government and his rage against the oppression
of minorities. In 1838, with the aid of the United States Army,
eighteen thousand Cherokee Indians were ruthlessly torn from
their homes in and near Georgia and sent to the region beyond
the Mississippi—despite their protests and despite evidence that
their progress toward civilization had been encouraging. When
word reached Emerson that the action was contemplated, he
wrote in his journal: "This sad disaster of the Cherokees, brought
to me by a sad friend to blacken my days and nights. I can do
nothing. Why shriek? Why strike ineffectual blows? I stir in it for
the sad reason that no other mortal will move, and if I do not,
why it is left undone. The amount of it, to be sure, is merely a
scream; but sometimes a scream is better than a thesis." Straight-
way he wrote a letter to the president of the United States, then
Martin Van Buren—a beautiful example of democracy in action.

Sir: The seat you fill places you in a relation of credit and near-
ness to every citizen. By right and natural position, every citizen
is your friend. Before any acts contrary to his own judgment or
interest have repelled the affections of any such man, each may
look with trust and living anticipation to your government. Each
has the highest right to call your attention to such subjects as are
of a public nature, and properly belong to the chief magistrate;
and the good magistrate will feel a joy in meeting such confidence.

Gentle enough! But here are a few sentences from the core of the
letter.

Such a dereliction of all faith and virtue, such a denial of justice, and such deafness to screams of mercy were never heard in
times of peace and in the dealing of a nation with its own allies

and wards, since the earth was made. Sir, does this government
think that the people of the United States are becoming savage
and mad? From their minds are the sentiments of love and good
nature wiped clean out? The soul of man, the justice, the mercy
that is the heart's heart in all men, from Maine to Georgia, does
abhor this business. . . . You, sir, will bring down that renowned
chair in which you sit into infamy if your seal is set to this instrument of perfidy.

Today it is the fashion to write letters to congressmen, instead of
the president—but that epistle is still a model.

Of course Emerson was opposed to slavery. In 1831, at a time
when an abolitionist was regarded in Boston as a dangerous
maniac, he lent his pulpit to an antislavery speaker, but he himself never joined an abolitionist society. "I like reform better than
its moulds," he concluded. Many of the more ardent opponents
of slavery regarded him as lukewarm, especially when he es-
poused freeing the slaves by buying them from their owners at
public expense. But the passage of the Fugitive Slave Law in 1850
forced him into the fray. That law made every man in Massachusetts liable to summons in aid of the return of escaped slaves, and
it had been passed with the outspoken advocacy of Daniel Webster, the political champion of the Bay State. In an address to the
people of Concord Emerson announced: "I have lived all my life
in this State, and never had any experience of personal inconve-
nience from the laws until now. They never came near me, to my
discomfort, before. But the Act of Congress of September 18,
1850, is a law which every one of you will break on the earliest
occasion,—a law which no man can obey or abet the obeying
without loss of self-respect and forfeiture of the name of a gentleman." In his private diary he had previously written, "I will not
obey it, by God!"

The problem of capital versus labor he considered, in its political connections at least, as the problem of property versus persons. Doubts, he noted, had already risen in his day "whether
too much weight had not been allowed in the laws to property,
and such a structure given to our usages as allowed the rich to
encroach on the poor, and keep them poor." Moreover, he felt

an "instinctive sense," obscure and inarticulate, "that the whole constitution of property," on its existing tenures, was injurious. Yet, he maintained, whatever action is taken, whatever the laws, persons and property both "must and will have their just sway." The boundaries of personal influence were in his eyes unlimited. But property also, he insisted, commands its power, for a cent is merely the representative of the necessities of human existence. "The law may in a mad freak say that all shall have power except the owners of property"; nevertheless "property will, year after year, write every statute that respects property." As for humanitarian legislation, Emerson was instinctively in favor of it. "Democratic institutions," he observed, "should be more thoughtful . . . for the welfare of sick and unable persons." The right to have employment, he believed, was—like the opportunity of civil rights, education, and free speech—a sacred obligation resting upon the state. But the right to acquire property and to maintain it was also a hallowed prerogative of the individual.

It is obvious that the essential basis of Emersonian democracy is far broader than mere nationality; the divine man is to be confined by no limits—certainly not by geographical limits. Emerson's generation prophesied American leadership for the world, even though it made little effort to provide a *modus operandi* that would insure a speedier realization of the prophecy. His essay called "The Fortune of the Republic" illustrates.

> It is not a question whether we shall be a multitude of people. No, that has been conspicuously decided already; but whether we shall be a new nation, the guide and lawgiver of all nations, as having clearly chosen and firmly held the simplest and best rule of political society. . . . I wish to see America not like the old powers of the earth, grasping, exclusive and narrow, but a benefactor such as no country ever was, hospitable to all nations, legislating for all nationalities. Nations were made to help each other as much as families were; and all advancement is by ideas, and not by brute force or mechanic force.

In the blundering kaleidoscope of international misapprehensions such noble sentiments sometimes have an odd way of focusing a pragmatic relevance to existence. They coerce by a kind of intrinsic authority. Is it heresy to suggest that our social engineering, both at home and abroad, needs an infusion of old-fashioned idealistic humanism, or that the Department of State might find a cluster of Emerson's democratic ideas as suitable for export as a thousand cases of florida water or a million bushels of wheat?

Nathaniel Hawthorne: Questioning Observer and Interpreter of America

ARLIN TURNER

In any attempt we make to re-create and to interpret earlier times, we like to supplement the facts and artifacts that have come down to us with the impressions and judgments of witnesses who experienced those times. It has seemed wise, as a rule, to seek out witnesses who were active in the affairs around them. Nathaniel Hawthorne has been thought not a dependable witness, since he presumably stood aside from the activities of his contemporaries. What could be learned about mundane affairs from an author who wrote tales entitled "The Prophetic Pictures" and "The Artist of the Beautiful," who created such unworldly characters as Arthur Dimmesdale in *The Scarlet Letter* and Aunt Hepzibah Pyncheon in *The House of the Seven Gables*, and who wrote a romance, *The Marble Faun*, which leaves unanswered, finally, the question whether one of the main characters has indeed the ears of a faun? How much reliance could be placed in a man who seemed more interested in the seventeenth century than in his own, who wrote about alchemy, witchcraft, and artists with prophetic powers, and whose focus was more on individual guilt than on the state of society or the course of the nation? Earlier in this century it was not uncommon to read in biographical or critical works that Hawthorne and his wife "took very slight interest in the questions which stirred New England life in their day and held entirely aloof from the reforms which shook the social life around them from center to foundation stone"; and that "in all his works there is to be found no trace of awareness of the contemporary physical world about him. He left . . . no records of the social life of his day."[1]

1. Hattie Tyng Griswold, *Home Life of Great Authors* (Chicago: A. C.

Such statements as these may serve at least the useful purpose
of reminding us that every age not only reinterprets earlier ages
by its own lights, but also, in a sense, remakes the past. These
views derived in part from Hawthorne's repeated avowal that his
was an isolated existence, such as he described in writing his
former college mate Henry Wadsworth Longfellow on June 4,
1837: "I have been carried apart from the main current of life,
and find it impossible to get back again. . . . I have made a captive of myself and put me into a dungeon; and now I cannot find
the key to let myself out—and if the door were open, I should be
almost afraid to come out." But such statements, we have learned,
have little basis in the facts of Hawthorne's life. To say that he
remained aloof from current reform efforts is to forget his commitment of himself and his savings to the communal Brook Farm
experiment. To say that he stood aside from the real world is to
forget that he was editor of a penny magazine, wrote a history of
the world for children, held appointments in the Boston customhouse and the Salem customhouse, proved himself a master of
political operation at the ward level, wrote the campaign biography for a successful presidential candidate, Franklin Pierce, took
a hand in Pierce's selection of political appointees, and served
four years as consul at Liverpool, the busiest post in the United
States foreign service.

Among our major authors, who else could offer such a list of
varied public activities? Who could know from personal engagement so much about the real world? Not Poe, Emerson, Thoreau,
Melville, Whitman, Mark Twain, Howells, and of course not
Henry James.

But how essential is an active role in public affairs to an understanding of what those affairs mean? A busy participant may
record what he observes and may report what he feels and thinks,
but he can hardly be expected to assess or even to see the entire
scene. The one best qualified as a historian of his own time may

---

McClurg, 1913), 211; John Albert Macy (ed.), *American Writers on American
Literature* (New York: Liveright, 1931), 98. See also Newton Arvin, *Haw-
thorne* (Boston: Little, Brown, 1929), 127, 177, and H. S. Canby, *Classic
Americans* (New York: Harcourt, Brace, 1931), 232.

be one who stands aloof, like the narrator in Hawthorne's sketch "Sights from a Steeple," who rises above the dust and noise at ground level and achieves something of the distance, along with the objectivity and the balance, that a historian must have. It may be that a recorder is most perceptive when he is least involved.

Aside from his engagement in public activities, including his dozen years in political appointments and his lifelong association with politicians and men of affairs, Hawthorne had other experiences and additional sources of knowledge that prepared him to understand the America of his time and to see it, as he invariably did, against its past. For one thing, his ancestry included two different strands of the American population. In the Hawthorne line, which had come down in Salem from the first settlement, were prominent figures in the first two generations—William, who passed sentences on the early Quakers, and his son John, who was a magistrate in the witch trials of 1692. Although Hawthorne took shame upon himself on account of these first two American ancestors, or at least said he did, he nevertheless asserted in his sketch "The Custom House" that, so far as he knew, his Hawthorne ancestry had "never been disgraced by a single unworthy member." He took reserved pride in his grandfather, who was of the fifth American generation, a sea captain, a hero in the Revolutionary War, and the subject of a popular ballad, and in his father, also a sea captain, who sailed in the fabulous early trade with the Orient.

Hawthorne's mother's family, the Mannings, came to the New World almost as early as the Hawthornes, but they were tradesmen and had left few marks on the public records. His grandfather (designated yeoman in a legal document at the time of his death) was a blacksmith endowed with energy and initiative, who became successively a livery stable operator, a stagecoach owner, and a trader and developer of new lands, as the population expanded and moved inland from the port towns. The Mannings were self-made, self-educated, and self-sufficient. The novelist's Uncle Robert Manning became internationally known as a pomologist and was honored in his own country.

Hawthorne was thoughtfully aware of the two strands of his

ancestry. When he was four years old, following the death of his father, his mother moved with him and his two sisters from the Hawthorne household to the Manning household. Several members of the Manning family recognized his special talents, even in his boyhood, with a perception not always present among those responsible for literary geniuses when they are young. They decided he should be educated, and from something less than modest means they sent him to Bowdoin College and after his graduation supported him through twelve years of apprenticeship to literature. It was only after he was graduated from college and was searching in colonial New England history for the materials of authorship that he encountered the Hawthorne ancestors who caused him to feel both shame and pride.

While Hawthorne lived as a boy on the Manning land in Maine, he moved comfortably among the down East backwoodsmen, and "savagized," as he said, in the uncut forests on the shore of Lake Sebago. From college classmates who would remain his close friends were to come a president of the United States, members of Congress, and a poet of international fame. A resident later of Boston, Concord, and the Berkshires of western Massachusetts, he had as neighbors some of the leading authors of the time, including Emerson, Thoreau, Melville, Margaret Fuller, Bronson Alcott, and George Bancroft; and at Brook Farm, among his companions in shoveling manure and hoeing corn were some of the most devoted transcendental idealists in a transcendental era. Even so, the ones whose company Hawthorne sought most readily, the ones he met at Parker's Saloon and Restaurant in Boston, were none of these, but instead were his customhouse associates, who scarcely knew that he was a literary author.

It was a lifelong purpose of Hawthorne's to observe the world around him—partly to gather the materials of literature and partly to satisfy an inveterate interest of his in human conduct and human character. As a young man he liked to travel incognito, slipping unobtrusively into an inn or a boardinghouse and observing the passengers on a stagecoach, the travelers from abroad, and the populous immigrant families on a canal boat or a Lake

Ontario steamboat. He filled his literary notebook with the manners, speech, and character of those he encountered; he sought also to sense and understand his America, to know its sources, its varieties and contrasts, and to foresee its future. His was a well-stocked mind in which to analyze the national character.

Hawthorne possessed habits of mind, moreover, that equipped him for acute observation. Skeptical and questioning in outlook, he avoided enthusiasm, choosing the middle ground as a rule and regularly asking whether there might not be another side, another way of looking at something before him, a different conclusion from the one most general among his associates. Social and public issues appealed to him especially if they furnished suitable contexts for exploring the moral and psychological dimensions of individual character. And those who knew him spoke often of his independence of mind and his absolute integrity. Herman Melville, who knew him in person and in his books, sent him on April 16, 1851, a letter in the form of a review of *The House of Seven Gables*, in which he declared, in a passage much quoted: "There is the grand truth about Nathaniel Hawthorne. He says No! in thunder; but the Devil himself cannot make him say *yes.* . . . He may perish; but so long as he exists he insists upon treating with all Powers upon an equal basis."

Hawthorne's was a mind to discover meanings everywhere, to see everything as symbol, not excluding his own thoughts and actions. A universe without unity and consistency could not make sense to him; nothing was without consequences; everything was related to everything else, however tenuously. History, therefore, was a continuum in which no individual or single episode could be understood alone. In this, as in other aspects of transcendental thought, he accepted as much as he found useful and avoided pushing on to conclusions that he thought false in Emerson, Thoreau, and others of his contemporaries. He chose to write about America, at a time when such a choice needed to be defended, as Henry Wadsworth Longfellow had done in his graduation address at Bowdoin College. When Hawthorne remarked once that New England was "quite as large a lump of earth" as his heart could "really take in," he was setting himself a practical limit to an area in which his own roots were planted and which he could hope to comprehend.[2] Everywhere he went in his travels, inside the bounds of New England or beyond, he saw the present as an outgrowth of the past.

Coincident with Hawthorne's beginning to write fiction, the colonial history in which his ancestors had made indelible marks was being reassessed by others around him. Early accounts of the witchcraft episode were republished, three of them in Salem. In this reassessment the early colonists did not fare well; it showed them stern, narrow, cruel, and generally benighted. This revisionist interpretation of early history might have given Hawthorne a simple portrait in dark monochrome for the early Puritans. But he was habitually fearful of simplifications. Human motives and human nature are too complex, he believed, to be portrayed in one shade. Hence the characters and the groups of characters we encounter on his pages—whether colonials or Royalists; Puritans, Quakers, Anglicans, or Shakers; alchemists or even witches—appear in shades of gray, rather than white or black, for such was his view of men and of their social organizations as well.

For all the use he made of historical facts, characters, and general background, Hawthorne's purpose was not to write historical romances or novels of manners. His interest was not in showing what life was like at a given time or "in those strange old times," but rather in showing—or assuming—that the seeds of one age produce fruit in a later age, that there is no escaping an inheritance, that the sins of the father are visited on the sons. His works enclose American history from the earliest settlements to his own time—primarily the history of New England, of Massachusetts, of Boston and Salem—and in the total there comes across an interpretation of the national character, experience, and prospects. It is an unquestioned assumption of his that the nation will flourish—its main characteristics being growth, development, and refinement—but only at a rate within the limits of man's capabilities.

2. Nathaniel Hawthorne to Horatio Bridge, January 15, 1857, in Horatio Bridge, *Personal Recollections of Nathaniel Hawthorne* (New York: Harper and Brothers, 1893), 155.

I have said that to Hawthorne's mind every act has its ines-capable effects. His tales and romances are populated with char-acters who demonstrate the inevitability of consequences. His own family in America illustrated the same iron necessity of cause and effect—so at least he liked to say, in repeating the mistaken report that a curse had been pronounced on one of his ancestors and in asserting that the effects of the curse reached down to his own time. In *The House of the Seven Gables* he constructed the history of the Pyncheon family to dramatize the weight of in-herited guilt on successive generations.

As with an individual and a family, so with a community. A town, a state, or a nation can have no significance apart from its past and its prospects for the future. And Hawthorne rarely em-ploys in his fiction a scene or an episode without displaying the historical antecedents and without offering speculations, implicit if not explicit, on the future that will ensue. He liked to scan the vistas of history, as in the sketch entitled "Main Street," which traces a street in Salem from the time it was but an Indian trail down almost to the present. Another sketch, "A Rill from the Town Pump," reaches back into early history when there was only a spring where the pump now stands on a busy street in Salem.

The story "The Gray Champion" supplements its plot with a projection into subsequent history. The Champion, of unspecified identity but by implication one of the judges who pronounced the sentence of death on King Charles I, came forward to challenge the royal governor and thus prevented the spilling of blood that seemed inevitable as the royal authority faced the colonials in the street. The story concludes with a prophetic glimpse of the future.

I have heard, that whenever the descendants of the Puritans are to show the spirit of their sires, the old man appears again. When eighty years had passed, he walked once more in King Street. Five years later, in the twilight of an April morning, he stood on the green, beside the meeting-house, at Lexington. . . . And when our fathers were toiling at the breastwork on Bunker's Hill, all through that night the old warrior walked his rounds. Long, long may it be, ere he comes again! His hour is one of darkness, and adversity, and peril. But should domestic tyranny oppress us, or the invader's step pollute our soil, still may the Gray Champion come.

Thus Hawthorne viewed the stretch of history in the same way he viewed the lifetime of a person he knew or a character in his fiction. No society could grow from a void; it too must have ancestors. The Puritan settlements, he pointed out more than once, were pieces of the Old World transplanted to the New.[3] All the more surely, any settlement of a later date would be that earlier settlement, as modified by forces that can be isolated and evaluated. He could accept Crèvecoeur's conclusion that the New World made of an American a different man from the one who had sailed west across the Atlantic; he once cited a report that near Biloxi, Mississippi, a settlement of gypsies who had emigrated from Europe lost all their hereditary characteristics as gypsies and were undistinguishable from other immigrants from their home country.[4] But to his mind the shaping of individual character, or the growth of the national character, was not a sudden miracle, but rather was the growth normal to man, taking its direction from the special concatenation of circumstances: land, people, history, and social, intellectual, and moral forces. In phrasing that pleased him and his wife, "Man's accidents are God's purposes."

Hawthorne had little to say about the frontier experience in America, about the individual, social, and political effects as civilization in his own time moved westward—less than William Cullen Bryant, whose actual world was limited to Massachusetts and New York, but who was fascinated by the land and the peoples of the western prairies; less than Irving, Cooper, Simms, and Parkman, of course; less than his Concord neighbor Henry David Thoreau, who had a lifetime hobby of condemning society and drew speculative conclusions about the proper symbolic direction

---

3. See "Main Street," for example, and the sketches entitled "Old News."
4. Nathaniel Hawthorne, "American Gipsies," *American Magazine of Useful and Entertaining Knowledge*, II (1836), 392; reprinted in Arlin Turner (ed.), *Hawthorne as Editor* (Baton Rouge: Louisiana State University Press, 1941), 243–44.

to take in going for a walk (he should walk southwest); less than Poe, who had never been west of the Shenandoah Valley of Virginia but wrote a book-length narrative of western exploration; less than even his friends the Boston Brahmins, Lowell and Holmes. There is evidence that Hawthorne read what was being published about the half-horse, half-alligator comic actors of the Mississippi River flatboats and that he knew the frontier romances of Cooper and Simms (though we have his word for it, in the sketch "Our Evening Party Among the Mountains," that he abhorred an Indian story). But he did not analyze the frontier as an idea or as a distinct state in the development of the nation—for the reason that he saw the frontier stage as common to all settlements, beginning with the earliest seaboard colonies; and in most of his fiction and his sketches the frontier stage is caught in the sweep of his glance backward. He may deal with the earliest colonial years, as in the sketch of Anne Hutchinson, or may move forward almost a century, as in "Roger Malvin's Burial"; in *The Scarlet Letter*, which spans a generation when the Massachusetts Bay Colony was only a quarter of a century old, the scene, the public officials and public affairs, and the way of life are presented with a faithfulness to detail possible only because the author was steeped in early colonial history. Even so, the focus is less on the external, public situation than on the psychological responses of characters placed in the particular circumstances provided in colonial Boston.

While constructing historical frames for his character studies, as in *The Scarlet Letter*, Hawthorne was ready to study the persons and the issues he encountered, and to record his assessments. And as his subjects moved closer to his own time, he was more inclined to offer such assessments. Wherever he dealt with facets of the developing nation, from the first settlements onward, he looked with the questioning glance that was habitual with him. He normally recognized contending forces, both current and historical, and he more often than not arrived at questions rather than clear answers, leaving the reader to balance in his own mind the meanings and values brought to his attention.

Although Hawthorne set the action of some of his tales no

more exactly than "in the olden times," he often indicated an exact date; and he wanted the reader to share his awareness of the historical orientation. He knew the historical sources for his lump of earth, New England, and he had a lively antiquarian interest; but he read the history from 1620 onward as an ingredient of the national character and as an annotation on the America of his time. That history, as he read it, defied the simplification he often encountered; it argued for the same complexity he found in individual human nature. In writing about people and events at intervals in the past, he sought a view that would be reconcilable in the entire span of American history.

Several conflicts recorded in American history gave Hawthorne evidence that the records of societies, no less than the records of individual lives, must take account of conflicting forces and divergent values. The earliest of the conflicts he recounted was between the Massachusetts Bay Colony and the Anglican settlement headed by Thomas Morton at Merry Mount. Keeping alive in the wilderness the hereditary sports and pastimes of Old England, the Merry Mounters were dancing about the maypole one summer day, the occasion being the marriage of the Lord and the Lady of the May. The dancing was interrupted, the story continues, when a band of Puritans arrived, "most dismal wretches, who said their prayers before daylight, and then wrought in the forest or the cornfield till evening made it prayer time again. . . . Woe to the youth or maiden who did but dream of a dance!" If there was dancing, "it was round the whipping-post, which might be termed the Puritan Maypole."

With the contrast thus established by "authentic passages from history," in Hawthorne's phrasing, the story moves to its resolution, bearing out the imagery of light and dark, of sunbeams and dark clouds. When the rioters had been scattered and the maypole had been cut down, the commander of the intruding band, the "Puritan of Puritans," John Endicott, "lifted the wreath of roses from the ruin of the Maypole, and threw it, with his own gauntleted hand, over the heads of the Lord and Lady of the May. It was a deed of prophecy. . . . They went heavenward, supporting each other along the difficult path which it was their lot to tread, and never wasted one regretful thought on the vanities of Merry Mount." Endicott, "the severest Puritan of all who laid the rock foundation of New England," had softened in their presence; and they had realized that they "had no more a home at Merry Mount." As Hawthorne interpreted this episode, the Puritans were capable of founding a new nation; the Merry Mounters were not. The light and the dark of the imagery had blended into gray.

Another early conflict set Puritans against Puritans. At the time Hawthorne was writing, the bonds of earlier theological strictness were being loosened, and sympathy would flow to Roger Williams and Anne Hutchinson, who were expelled because of deviant doctrinal tenets. In the opening chapter of *The Scarlet Letter* Hawthorne refers to "the sainted Anne Hutchinson," but in an earlier sketch he severely qualified her sainthood. She lived in "an era when liberality was not esteemed a Christian virtue," he wrote, and when many of those around her were "ready to propagate the religion of peace by violence." Among them was John Endicott, "who would stand with his drawn sword at the gate of heaven, and resist to the death all pilgrims thither, except they travelled his own path." But it was an era "in which religious freedom was wholly inconsistent with public safety," as Hawthorne phrased it, and to have allowed a breach in the total unity of belief through a diversity of sects would have cost their survival. He remarked further that Mrs. Hutchinson's religious views were no less narrow and no less intolerantly asserted than those of John Cotton and others of the dominant group.

A third conflict occurred within the first American generation, in the time of Hawthorne's first American ancestor. The Quakers came in 1656, asserting that their light within took precedence over Biblical revelation, insisting that they were emissaries of God, called to chastise both church and state, and refusing to acknowledge civil authority. When progressively harsher sentences on them proved to no avail, a law was passed providing for banishment on pain of death; and in 1659 "the government

of Massachusetts Bay indulged two members of the Quaker sect
with the crown of martyrdom." Such is Hawthorne's phrasing in
his story "The Gentle Boy."

Again, sympathy is with the persecuted—the martyred Quaker,
his child, called the Gentle Boy, and the Puritan who has be-
friended the child and later comes to embrace Quakerism. Yet
there are reminders throughout the tale that something is to be
said on the other side. The Quakers sought martyrdom and refused to be denied. They defied laws and conventions, forced
their way to the pulpits of the Puritan churches and harangued
the congregation, went naked into the churches and through the
streets. And they denied human affections and responsibilities, as
Catherine, the mother of the Gentle Boy, does when she aban-
dons her child to the direst possibilities, under the spell of fanaticism, which Hawthorne never failed to condemn. Finally, the
antagonisms have lessened. The fanaticism of the Quakers has
paled; Catherine lives in the home of the Puritan who turned
Quaker, and they seem to be reconciled in a peaceful middle
ground. But a final glance at the community leaves the reader
with a Hawthornean reminder that permanent residence in a
middle ground is not to be expected, and with also an ironic
thrust at the Puritans, who have prevailed in the conflict between
two forces of bigotry and fanaticism. When Catherine had become a familiar figure in the community, we read, she was "a
being on whom the otherwise superfluous sympathies of all might
be bestowed. Everyone spoke of her with that degree of pity
which it is pleasant to experience; every one was ready to do her
the little kindnesses which are not costly, yet manifest good will;
and when at last she died, a long train of her once bitter persecutors followed her, with decent sadness and tears that were not
painful, to her place by Ilbrahim's green and sunken grave."

It is worth noting that as "The Gentle Boy" first appeared in
1832, it recited "extenuating circumstances" for the conduct of
the Puritans that were "more numerous than can generally be
pleaded by persecutors." In reprinting the tale in 1837, the author
omitted much of this apology for the Puritans, perhaps giving less
thought than at first to William Hathorne, his "grave, bearded,

sable-cloaked and steeple-crowned progenitor who came so early with his Bible and his sword" (as he is characterized in "The Custom House") and who is recorded as pronouncing sentence on three Quaker women. Hawthorne was perhaps also thinking less about the social, public issue and more about the nature and experiences of the individual characters.

The witch hangings of 1692 occurred in the lifetime of Hawthorne's second American ancestor, John Hathorne, who was a principal actor in that sad drama, and on whose account Hawthorne took greatest shame upon himself. Witchcraft furnished him impressive representational materials for literary use such as he found, for example, in the lore of alchemy. In the tale entitled "Alice Doane's Appeal" an inner story of wizardry and Gothic mystery from the old witch times is read aloud by its author on Gallows Hill, in order to observe his own response and the response of his listeners—the response, that is, of one age to an earlier age. "We are a people of the present," the author of the witch story asserts, "and till a year or two since . . . it was not every citizen of our ancient town that could tell, within half a century, so much as the date of the witchcraft delusion." But he has himself "often coveted the historical influence of the spot" where the witches were hanged.

Hawthorne offers no extenuation for the sad errors of that earlier time, as he offers for the persecutors of the Quakers; but he enters one demurrer to the view of the witchcraft episode which was developing among his contemporaries. He came to see, not that there had been a spontaneous eruption in the masses, but that the delusion had been initiated and maintained by the learned men of the community—the Reverend Samuel Parris of Salem Village, the Reverend Nicholas Noyes of the First Church of Salem, and the Reverend Cotton Mather, probably the most erudite man in the colony, who came from Boston to observe and to assist at the trials and the hangings. Hawthorne referred to Cotton Mather often: calling him the man who "hung the witches" ("Time's Portraiture"), "the chief instigator of the mischief" of the witchcraft delusion (*Grandfather's Chair*), and the "one bloodthirsty man" involved in the witchcraft proceedings, and recounting—from histories of the hangings—how George Burroughs, former minister of the Salem Village church, addressed the assemblage from the steps of the scaffold to such effect that after he had been hanged, Mather felt the need to ride forward on his horse and overcome the doubts that had arisen among the people, so that the other hangings of the afternoon could proceed ("Main Street"). Alongside the learned and venomous Cotton Mather, the populace might be assigned less of the blame for the hangings. So it seemed to Hawthorne's questioning mind; he was unwilling to be swept along into emotional or faddish views, such as prevailed either in the old witch times or in his own revisionist times.

In one after another of his historical and biographical sketches and often in his fiction, Hawthorne turned his questioning gaze on some aspect of the American experience. As he traveled about New England and into Canada and westward at least as far as Detroit to store his mind and his notebook with the materials of fiction, he interrupted his recording only now and then to set down his interpretations. There is evidence, however, in what he chose to record and in occasional supplementary comment, that his usual habits of mind prevailed. The travel sketch entitled "On an Ontario Steamboat" describes the three classes represented on board, with special note taken of the immigrants, "the exiles of another clime—the scum which every wind blows off the Irish shores—the pauper dregs which England flings out upon America." He speculated, as he observed the crowded deck, as to what degrading experiences were theirs on their travels from the Old World, and what the effects would be on individuals and on families. Thus he sounded a note heard wherever the Irish were streaming off the ships to become the laborers on the canals and the railroads and the household servants of New England—a note he later heard among his neighbors at Concord, where the Irish laborers on the Fitchburg Railroad occupied crowded shanties on the shore of Walden Pond. It was in character for Hawthorne to pass beyond that simplistic view and to add a twofold affirmation in his statement that "nothing short of settled depravity could resist the strength of moral influences diffused throughout our native land (that stock of homebred virtue is large enough to absorb and neutralize so much of foreign vice), and that the outcasts of Europe, if not by their own choice, yet by an almost inevitable necessity, promote the welfare of the country that receives them to its bosom."

Although Hawthorne had little tolerance for the reform agitation that permeated his time—temperance reform, women's rights, prison reform, the abolition of capital punishment, the abolition of slavery, the equalization of wealth, and various types of communal living—he went to Brook Farm with "faith and force enough to form generous hopes of the world's destiny," to quote the character in *The Blithedale Romance* who seems to voice the author's views on this matter, and to do what in him "lay for their accomplishment." But he left the community after six months, before its constitution was revised to declare without equivocation, "the divine order is closer than is generally supposed," and "humanity . . . is at length prepared to enter into that universal order toward which it has perpetually moved." Reform of any significance, he thought, must be moral reform, which he often phrased as the purification of the human heart. He was firm in judging the common run of reform efforts, saying, "There is no instance, in all history, of the human will and intellect having perfected any great moral reform by methods which it adapted to that end; but the progress of the world, at every step, leaves some evil or wrong on the path behind it, which the wisest of mankind, of their own set purpose, could never have found the way to rectify." [5]

Hawthorne's impatience with shallow or misguided reform movements had an offsetting devotion to genuine reform. While United States consul at Liverpool, he was a faithful public servant and, moreover, undertook to bring about reform where he found the need great and thought there was some chance of improvement. Before he had been long in the consulate, he was convinced that "Hell itself" could be no worse than some of the American merchant ships. The crews included only a few Americans; they

5. Nathaniel Hawthorne, *Life of Franklin Pierce* (Boston: Ticknor, Reed, and Fields, 1852), 113–14.

were made up of the "off-scourings and refuse of all the seaports of the world"; and the mates were not likely to be much better.[6] He noted a bitter irony, in writing to his sister-in-law Elizabeth Peabody, herself an inveterate reformer: philanthropists had secured the abolition of flogging in the merchant marine and had thus deprived the captain of all authority to enforce discipline.[7] The result was that the mates resorted to surreptitious, barbarous means of getting the work of the ship done; and one ship after another brought into Liverpool harbor a history of appalling abuses, including murder; but because of inadequate treaties most cases fell between the British and the American courts, and few of the criminals were brought to justice.

Hawthorne used all his consular authority—and sometimes stretched his authority—to correct abuses. He urged President Pierce, the secretary of state, and his friend Senator Charles Sumner to take up the matter; he supported the English societies and politicians who tried to work through the British government. He prayed for "some New Englander, with the itch of reform in him," to "turn his thoughts this way."[8] An immediate first step, he thought, should be to legalize flogging temporarily; subsequent major steps would come through revisions of laws and international agreements and through a long-range plan for recruiting and training American seamen.

Hawthorne was so distressed at the opening of the Civil War that he could not write as usual—there would have been "a kind of treason," he said, "in insulating one's self from the universal fear and sorrow." In his essay "Chiefly about War Matters," published in the *Atlantic Monthly* for July, 1862, following a trip to Washington, he considered a kind of token participation in

6. Randall Stewart (ed.), *The English Notebooks of Nathaniel Hawthorne* (New York: Russell and Russell, 1941), 267; see Hawthorne's *Our Old Home* (Columbus: Ohio State University Press, 1970), Chapter 1, Vol. V of 13 vols., in William Charvat, *et al.* (eds.), *Centenary Edition of the Works of Nathaniel Hawthorne*.

7. Hawthorne to Elizabeth Peabody, October 8, 1857, in Berg Collection, New York Public Library; printed in part in Rose Hawthorne Lathrop, *Memories of Hawthorne* (Boston: Houghton, Mifflin, 1898), 337.

8. Stewart (ed.), *The English Notebooks of Nathaniel Hawthorne*, 267.

the great struggle. He and his wife had championed Daniel Webster when to do so was to stand apart from their neighbors in Massachusetts. In writing the campaign biography of Franklin Pierce, he had been able to endorse Pierce's views on the growing sectional tension, for they were his views also. He had been impatient with the abolitionists for the same reason as with the enthusiasts in other causes. In writing about the war matters that came under his view in the nation's capital, he displayed his lifelong habit of questioning, his usual reluctance to accept a view that others around him championed with more enthusiasm than thought.

Because this essay was being published in wartime, Hawthorne realized that he must restrain his normal inclination to look at two sides instead of one and to question positions generally held. In sending the manuscript on May 7 to James T. Fields, who had been his editor and publisher since *The Scarlet Letter*, he remarked that he had affixed "editorial footnotes," which he hoped Fields would adopt, "they being very loyal." He had found it difficult, he added, "not to lapse into treason continually," but he had "made manful resistance to the temptation." The footnotes pretended that the editor was objecting at several points, for example, to a remark that state loyalties made it necessary for a southern resident to commit treason against either his state or the national government. He wondered how citizens of Massachusetts would respond to the presence of southern troops in the state. In a similar vein he noted that, following its famous voyage, the *Mayflower* became a slave ship. Fields accepted the footnotes but objected to the account of Hawthorne's visit to the White House and his description of President Lincoln. Hawthorne answered on May 23 that he thought Fields wrong but would comply, and added, "What a terrible thing it is to try to let off a little bit of truth into this miserable humbug of a world! If I had sent you the article as I conceived it, I should not so much have wondered."

Late in 1863 Lincoln's military adviser, General Ethan Allen Hitchcock, wrote acquaintances of his at Concord, asking opinions on a proposal he feared was gaining support in Washington, that a policy of retaliation against Confederate prisoners be adopted, the justification being reports that captured Union soldiers were underfed and mistreated in southern prisons. Sophia Hawthorne replied to General Hitchcock in a long letter of November 16, reiterating her exclamation, "No retaliation of any kind! . . . To hang or even shoot innocent men because others over whom we have no control may have committed wrongs, seems to me a deliberate sin." Earlier she had stated her belief "that God's law would without fail have removed slavery without this dreadful convulsive action. It always seems to me that Man is very arrogant in taking such violent measures to *help God* who needs no help. . . . I find no one in Concord or hardly in Boston to whom I can utter such sentiments without exciting fiery indignation. My sisters cannot hear me speak a word. They believe alone in instant vengeance on the slave owner. . . . To my husband only I can speak. He is very all-sided and can look serenely on opposing forces and do justice to each." She could report that her husband was entirely of her opinion as to retaliation, and that he was surprised to learn that Emerson had joined Mary Mann in favoring retaliation. Hawthorne was so surprised, in fact, that he called on Emerson and was assured that he did not agree with Mary Mann. Mrs. Hawthorne wrote Hitchcock in haste on November 22 to correct what she had said, and added, "Mr. Emerson has used so many *ifs* in talking to my sister, that in effect he differs from her, while she is deceived by the *ifs*." [9]

Hawthorne was not one to equivocate with *ifs*, nor one to be intimidated by Ralph Waldo Emerson, assuredly not one to follow the crowd thoughtlessly and add his voice to the clamor. He gave little satisfaction to enthusiasts advocating causes, or to those who came with emotional readings of American history or simplistic resolutions of current issues. When he was among associates—at a meeting of the Saturday Club in Boston, which he attended occasionally, at Emerson's house, at dinner parties while consul at Liverpool—it was his habit, while conversation proceeded among the others, to sit only half-facing them and to

9. Sophia Hawthorne to Ethan Allen Hitchcock, November 22, 1863, in Manuscript Division, Library of Congress.

divide his attention between the conversation and his own thoughts. The others present on such occasions, if they had read his books, would have the uneasy feeling that he was subjecting them to the same probing with which he studied his fictional characters. The senior Henry James once spent his time during a meeting of the Saturday Club chiefly in observing Hawthorne and, aware of current affairs—this was January, 1861—wrote afterward, "The old world is breaking up on all hands—the glimpse of the everlasting granite I caught in Hawthorne shows me that there is stock enough for fifty better." [10]

For all his reclusiveness, real or feigned, for all his habit of observing rather than joining the currents that stirred the nation in his time, for all his tendency to demur and to see more than one side, Hawthorne succeeded in asking useful questions, as a rule, and in provoking thought in his readers, whether on a subject in early history or in contemporary America, viewed against that history. The breadth and the earnestness of his observation, together with the intellectual and moral integrity that Herman Melville and others of his contemporaries found in him, are assurance that the quality of his guidance to an understanding of the national experience and the national character would be determined only by his perception; his fictional penetration into other areas of human history and human nature is testimony that his perception was considerable.

10. Edward Waldo Emerson, *The Early Years of the Saturday Club, 1855–1870* (Boston: Houghton, Mifflin, 1918), 331–32.

The 1850s:
The First Afro-American
Literary Renaissance

WILLIAM L. ANDREWS

The efflorescence of creativity in fiction and poetry during the 1920s in Harlem has been termed traditionally the first renaissance in Afro-American letters. But if Langston Hughes was right in 1926 when he singled out the driving force behind the New Negro renaissance as black artists' determination "to express our individual dark-skinned selves without fear or shame," then this renaissance should be recognized as a rebirth of a spirit of artistic self-reliance and creative autonomy that was the legacy of an earlier generation of Afro-American writers.[1] During the much-celebrated American renaissance of the 1850s, the age of Emerson and Whitman, the first group of black American men of letters also produced a body of literature and, perhaps more important, a set of precedents and traditions that subsequent generations of writers could build on. Emerson, Thoreau, Hawthorne, Melville, and Whitman have been remembered for both their individual achievements and their collective sponsorship of a new American confidence in its own artistic potential and perspective. On the other hand, those who helped to instill a parallel kind of romantic spirit and ethnic awareness in Afro-American literature have either been largely forgotten or dissociated from their roles in this important movement in black American literary history. The purpose of this essay is to identify the major work of the first Afro-American literary renaissance and to explain its relationship to some aspects of mid-nineteenth-century American romantic thought.

1. Langston Hughes, "The Negro Artist and the Racial Mountain," *Nation*, CXXII (June 23, 1926), 694.

Afro-American literature of the 1850s has not been read in a specifically romantic context heretofore, probably because its contribution to belletristic literature was comparatively small.[2] Those mid-century black writers who ventured into poetry, for instance, seem to have been carried there more by social and political fervor than by the muse. This in itself testifies to the presence of a romantic-reformist impulse among such early versifiers as James M. Whitfield or Frances E. W. Harper. But powerfully expressed abolitionist sentiments alone could not inspire a distinctive Afro-American poetic mode. There being no drama by a black writer before 1858, the burden of innovation and black artistic expression in the 1850s fell on the prose narrative, which, in the particular form of the fugitive-slave narrative, had already taken a place of some prominence among liberal-minded readers of the North.[3]

The fugitive-slave narrative evolved from popular narrative traditions of the eighteenth century, particularly the Protestant spiritual autobiography and conversion narrative, the captivity narrative, and travel-writing genres. Through the words of pioneering black autobiographers—Briton Hammon, James Gronniosaw, John Marrant, Olaudah Equiano, Richard Allen, and Venture Smith—the earliest first-person accounts of slave life in America came to the attention of whites in England and America.[4] Not all of these stories spoke out against the evils of slavery.

2. For a general look at the slave narrative's historical significance, see Edward Margolies' "Ante-Bellum Slave Narratives: Their Place in American Literary History," *Studies in Black Literature*, IV (Autumn, 1973), 1–8, and Frances Smith Foster's *Witnessing Slavery: The Development of Ante-Bellum Slave Narratives* (Westport, Conn.: Greenwood, 1979), 142–54.

3. The first play written by an Afro-American was William Wells Brown's *The Escape; or, a Leap for Freedom*, a five-act drama first published in Boston in 1858.

4. See *Narrative of the Uncommon Suffering and Surprizing Deliverance of Briton Hammon, a Negro Man-servant to General Winslow, of Marshfield* (Boston: Green & Russell, 1760), *A Narrative of the Most Remarkable Particulars in the Life of James Albert Ukawsaw Gronniosaw, an African Prince, as Related by Himself* (Bath, England: S. Hazard, 177[?]), *A Narrative of the Lord's Wonderful Dealings with John Marrant, a Black* (London: Gilbert & Plummer, 1785), *The Interesting Narrative of the Life of Olaudah Equiano, or Gustavus Vassa, the African* (2 vols.; London: the author, 1789), *The Life*

Marrant's *Narrative*, for example, gives no evidence of his being a slave and does not address the topic of chattel slavery. Hammon's tale of separation, capture, and joyful reunion with his Massachusetts owner implies a benevolent relationship between servant and master. By contrast, Equiano provided graphic portrayals of brutal conditions on West Indian plantations, and Allen spoke emphatically of his time in slavery as "a bitter pill, notwithstanding we had a good master." What unifies these early slave narratives is not an abolitionist purpose but a Christian perspective in which the slave pictures himself as a pilgrim passing through a world of sin and suffering. Accepting their lot as a trial prepared by God to test their faithfulness, these pioneering black narrators view themselves almost uniformly as dark-skinned counterparts of Bunyan's Mr. Christian, who must aggressively resist the "spiritual despotism" of sin, but may use only "honest means" to end their physical bondage to slavery.[5]

Not until after the split in abolitionist circles in the early 1830s and the rise of a new militancy in the antislavery movement did the slave narrative break out of the pacifistic, traditionally Protestant, and apolitical world view that had made it primarily a document which justified the ways of God to the black man. By the late 1830s slave narratives appeared under the authorship or dictation of ex-bondmen who claimed to have fled slavery through force or guile or both, with no apologies for choosing their "un-Christian" means of becoming free. Because their stories contained much firsthand evidence of the outrages and mundane workings of the slave system, the narratives of Moses Roper, Charles Ball, and James Williams were among the first seized upon by antislavery publishers in search of an arresting way to command the public ear.[6] Thus the fugitive-slave narra-

---

Experience and Gospel Labors of the Rt. Rev. Richard Allen (Philadelphia: Martin & Boden, 1833), and *A Narrative of the Life and Adventures of Venture, a Native of Africa: But Resident Above Sixty Years in the United States of America* (New London, Conn.: C. Holt, 1798).

5. The first quoted term is from Allen's *Life Experience and the Gospel Labors*; the latter is taken from *The Interesting Narrative of the Life of Olaudah Equiano*.

6. See the trend-setting *Narrative of the Adventures and Escape of Moses*

tive genre was born, its reason for being largely attributable to its usefulness as a propaganda weapon. Unfortunately, when such "slave narratives" as the *Memoirs of Archy Moore* (1836) and the *Narrative of James Williams* (1838) were revealed to be spurious, the veracity of the ex-slave was impugned and his literary gifts were doubted.[7] To disprove these conclusions, Frederick Douglass, a fugitive himself and an abolitionist lecturer of Garrisonian persuasion, wrote and published his own *Narrative of the Life of Frederick Douglass, an American Slave* in 1845. The unquestionable authenticity of detail, the emotional control, rhetorical skill, and lively characterizations in the *Narrative* made it famous, and Douglass' book became something of a model for other fugitive slaves to follow in recounting their lives. During the next five years, Douglass' precedent made possible the publication of at least a dozen fugitive-slave narratives, each of which presented its subject's life within a structural pattern that varied little, though many incidental differences remained. Like Douglass, these ex-slaves or, more often, their white amanuenses, began by describing their plantation origins, went on to recount their shocking initiations into hardship and suffering, pictured in striking detail their harrowing and suspenseful escapes, and concluded with their decisions in the North (or Canada) to serve God and man, usually through antislavery work.

It should not be surprising, therefore, that by the beginning of the 1850s, the fugitive-slave narrative had taken on a somewhat formulaic character. Although a William Wells Brown, a James W. C. Pennington, or a Henry Bibb could follow Douglass into print with self-authored stories that bore an individualistic stamp,

---

Roper, *from American Slavery* (London: Harvey and Darton, 1837), *Slavery in the United States: A Narrative of the Life and Adventures of Charles Ball, A Black Man* (Lewiston, Pa.: J. W. Shugert, 1836), and *Narrative of James Williams, An American Slave Who Was for Several Years a Driver on a Cotton Plantation in Alabama* (New York: American Anti-Slavery Society, 1838).

7. *The Slave; or, Memoirs of Archy Moore* (Boston: J. H. Eastburn, 1836) was offered to the public by its anonymous "editor" as a first-person account of an ex-slave. In 1839, its actual creator, Richard Hildreth, a white abolitionist, acknowledged his authorship. The *Narrative of James Williams* was judged false in a number of its details and was withdrawn from circulation by its publishers.

the dictations of men like Lewis G. Clarke (1845), Milton Clarke (1846), "Aaron" (1846?), Andrew Jackson (1847), Josiah Henson (1849), Henry "Box" Brown (1849), and Thomas Jones (1850) took on a somewhat generic cast when shaped into narrative form by abolitionist "editors."[8] The similarity of outline, incident, and tone among the majority of slave narratives in the late 1840s did not detract significantly from their propaganda function. However, the tendency toward standardization of black people's experiences and feelings in the fugitive-slave narrative, especially as it came from the hands of abolitionist transcribers and editors, necessitated by 1850 a period of generic experimentation, psychological candor, and assertion of the individual imagination among freemen who aspired to be literary spokesmen.

One of the major liabilities of the fugitive-slave narrative as a literary model stemmed from one of its strengths as a propaganda instrument. Fugitive-slave narrators felt constrained to concentrate largely on the *facts* of slavery. They were preoccupied with their own credibility, with being believed by white audiences. Frederick Douglass wrote his *Narrative*, not out of a desire to review his own remarkable life, but to prove that he was not an impostor when he claimed a firsthand knowledge of slavery. The *Narrative*, he said, was designed to disseminate "the leading facts connected with my experience in slavery, giving names of persons, places, and dates—thus putting it in the power of any who doubted, to ascertain the truth or falsehood of my story of being a fugitive slave."[9] Subsequent narrative writers were equally scrupulous in giving their readers only facts, verifiable if possible by reference to other sources. Slave narrative prefaces repeatedly declared that the ensuing narratives were free from

---

8. The *Narrative of William W. Brown, a Fugitive Slave* (Boston: Anti-Slavery Office, 1847), *The Fugitive Blacksmith; or, Events in the History of James W. C. Pennington* (2nd. ed.; London: C. Gilpin, 1849), and the *Narrative of the Life and Adventures of Henry Bibb, an American Slave* (New York: the author, 1849)—all rivaled Douglass' *Narrative of the Life of Frederick Douglass, an American Slave* (Boston: Anti-Slavery Office, 1845).

9. Frederick Douglass, *My Bondage and My Freedom* (New York: Miller, Orton, and Mulligan, 1855), 363.

exaggerations or embellishments by their authors. William Lloyd Garrison promised the readers of Douglass' story that they would find in it "nothing exaggerated, nothing drawn from the imagination."[10] Some ex-slaves like Linda Brent even insisted, "I have not exaggerated the wrongs inflicted by Slavery; on the contrary, my descriptions fall far short of the facts."[11] In the slave narrative, understating the facts was preferable to the suspicion of an overstatement or imaginative rendering of them. The possibility of doubts about their veracity caused many fugitives to buttress their stories with recommendatory prefaces and appended testimonials from white men affirming the author's trustworthiness. This overwhelmingly documentary character of the slave narrative, replete with its solicitation of white endorsements, stood as a major inhibition to imaginative creativity and artistic individualism among black writers at mid-century.

A further inhibition to a viable and independent Afro-American literature is illustrated in an anecdote that Douglass told for the first time in his second autobiography, *My Bondage and My Freedom* (1855), itself a major work of the black renaissance of the fifties. In the early 1840s, Douglass recalls, he was persuaded by Garrison and other abolitionists to give speeches that "were almost exclusively made up of narrations of my own personal experience as a slave." Because antislavery audiences said, "Let us have the facts," Douglass' colleagues "always wished to pin me down to my simple narrative." "Give us the facts," his superiors tell him; "we will take care of the philosophy." However, Douglass found that "it did not entirely satisfy me to *narrate* wrongs; I felt like *denouncing* them. . . . Besides, I was growing [intellectually], and needed room." Douglass' chafing at the bit of the simple slave narrative did not alter his mentors' assumptions about his identity and function on the platform, however. "Be yourself," the leader of the speaking team urged Douglass, "and tell your story."[12]

10. William Lloyd Garrison, Preface to the *Narrative of the Life of Frederick Douglass, an American Slave.*
11. Linda Brent, Preface to her *Incidents in the Life of a Slave Girl* (Boston: the author, 1861).
12. Douglass, *My Bondage and My Freedom*, 361–62.

Many of the same assumptions about the identity, capabilities, and usefulness of ex-slaves with stories to write and tell underlie the majority of the fugitive-slave narratives of the 1840s and 1850s. When fugitives collaborated, as they often had to, with abolitionists in the preparation of their narratives, they generally supplied a "statement of facts" which their editors then fashioned into narratives punctuated with abolitionist arguments. To what extent the ex-slaves would have interpreted the facts of their own lives in a way consistent with the interpretations of their editors remains, of course, unclear. What may be inferred, however, from reading many slave narratives is that the fugitive was consulted for the materials of the story but not for the "philosophy" that would explain their meaning. Black literary novices like William Wells Brown were praised by abolitionists when their narratives displayed "simplicity and ingenuousness," for these qualities carried with them "a conviction of the truthfulness of the picture."[13] Thus the fugitive-slave narrative as a popular literary genre, the only one in which black writers had achieved any fame, presented a no-win choice for most aspiring Afro-American literary people. A writer who had not been born a slave had no story to tell.[14] A former slave might yield to the pressure to give an unvarnished, simple recitation of his slave experiences and thereby strike a blow against the peculiar institution. But in so doing he was acceding to a kind of second-class literary citizenship, in which outside authorities judged the value and proper use of his literary resources. Once the slave narrative form and function were set, compromise of one's right to define one's individual black self and interpret one's experience freely became increasingly likely for writers of slave narratives in the 1850s.

These are some of the reasons why the 1850s saw considerable

13. J. C. Hathaway, Preface to the first edition of the *Narrative of William W. Brown.*
14. An exception was Solomon Northup, a free-born New Yorker, whose experience as a kidnapped slave in Louisiana was recounted in a ghostwritten narrative entitled *Twelve Years a Slave* (Auburn and Buffalo, New York: Derby, Orton, and Mulligan, 1853); for a reprinted edition, see Sue Eakin and Joseph Logsdon (eds.), *Twelve Years a Slave* (Baton Rouge: Louisiana State University Press, 1968).

experimentation in Afro-American prose narratives. The first to move beyond the fugitive-slave narrative form was William Wells Brown. After publishing four editions of his continually expanding *Narrative* in the late 1840s, Brown became in 1852 the first Afro-American writer to publish a travel book. Neither a resounding literary nor financial success, *Three Years in Europe* was, nevertheless, an important signal from a black writer.[15] Here was a personal narrative by an American ex-slave in which the antislavery theme was not featured. Instead Brown wrote descriptive sketches of picturesque and historical places and composed tributes to personages like the de Tocquevilles, Pope, and Burns. Brown's pen yielded few especially remarkable observations. What mattered was that, the expectations of abolitionist leaders notwithstanding, Brown decided that his subjective judgments and feelings on matters other than slavery were worth offering to the public.[16] *Three Years in Europe* was the first Afro-American narrative to proceed from the unprecedented assumption by a black author that telling his story need no longer require telling a story of slavery. This widening of the black writer's purview on experience and the asserting of the value of his subjective responses to experience gave a romantic impetus to the Afro-American literary renaissance.

Brown followed up his travel book with another first in Afro-American literature, the novel *Clotel; or, The President's Daughter* (1853).[17] The first novel by an Afro-American, *Clotel* bore a subtitle—*A Narrative of Slave Life in the United States*—which testified to its close relationship to the slave narrative genre. Brown's attempt to interweave several plots rather than to pursue the single autobiographical thread of the slave narrative glar-

15. William Wells Brown, *Three Years in Europe; or, Places I Have Seen and People I Have Met* (London: Charles Gilpin, 1852) enjoyed a modest sale and a friendly, if not enthusiastic, reading from the British press. See William Edward Farrison's *William Wells Brown, Author and Reformer* (Chicago: University of Chicago Press, 1969), 207–209.

16. Farrison, in *William Wells Brown*, notes that the leading British abolitionist of the day wanted "more anti-slavery matter, and less of what can be found in our 'guide books' & travelling companions" (p. 207).

17. William Wells Brown, *Clotel; or, The President's Daughter: A Narrative of Slave Life in the United States* (London: Partridge & Oakey, 1853).

ingly revealed his literary unsophistication. He borrowed heavily from abolitionist fiction for his plots and characters; he illustrated his exposition with numerous reports, advertisements, and commentary quoted from newspapers. As a result *Clotel* displays that lingering preoccupation with documenting the facts and adhering to the sources and sentiments of popular abolitionist writing that had already hampered the imaginative freedom of the fugitive-slave narrative.

On the other hand, *Clotel* was significant to the development of the Afro-American renaissance because it attempted to present a myth of American history within which the facts of contemporary American slavery could be interpreted. Brown prefaced his novel with the claim that "were it not for persons in high places owning slaves, and thereby giving the system a reputation, and especially professed Christians, Slavery would long since have been abolished." As a novelist, Brown would try to "fasten the guilt on those who move in a higher circle." The first chapter then identifies the two heroines of the novel, Clotel and Althesa, as the slave offspring of Thomas Jefferson, who Brown reminds his English reader was "the writer of the Declaration of American Independence, and one of the presidents of the great republic." Thus Jefferson becomes Brown's symbol for "persons in high places" who owned slaves and who lent the institution its republican respectability. Brown was not the only abolitionist who had heard the rumor of Jefferson's siring slave children, but he alone among abolitionist fiction writers turned this rumor into an informing myth whereby the tragic facts of American slavery could be seen in a political and historical, as well as sensationalistic, context. By making Jefferson the ultimate cause of all the tragic events in his novel, Brown could expose the archetypal American Democrat as a rank hypocrite and, via the same symbol, fasten the moral responsibility for the fate of Afro-Americans on American Democracy as personified in its progenitor-president. This revisionistic myth making, though Brown capitalized on it only slightly in *Clotel*, showed that the black writer of the 1850s had begun to render American reality not only according to objective facts but also in accordance with his subjective interpretation of the country's myths and symbols.

One of the more cherished of these myths contrasted the South, presented as a land of cruel captivity, with the North, seen as a haven of freedom for the Afro-American. The second Afro-American novel, Frank J. Webb's *The Garies and Their Friends* (1857), was to deny that sort of simplistic thinking among self-satisfied Yankees.[18] Tracing the fortunes of two Afro-American families in Philadelphia, Webb's novel proved that racial discrimination impinged on virtually all phases of life in the North. Webb took pains to reveal the notion of black inferiority in the minds of all classes of northern whites, ranging from a respectable minister who refuses to officiate at a mixed marriage through white workers who participate in mob action against blacks. Despite its contrived happy ending, *The Garies and Their Friends* offered little hope for reform of northern racism. Its purpose seems to have been to render in substantial and depressing detail what the fugitive-slave narrative had usually sketched in optimistic generalities—the condition of the freeman in the North.

Clotel and *The Garies and Their Friends* served as complementary exposés of the nature and extent of racism in the American South and North. Each novel relied overmuch on the devices, diction, and formal elements of popular sentimental fiction, but both incorporated a kind of sensationalistic realism when treating the extremes of American racial conditions—a realism that helped to counterbalance the stock romanticism of their plots. Both Brown and Webb were engaged principally in enlarging the boundaries of the Afro-American fictive world and shedding the point of view of the traditional Afro-American narrative voice, that of the untutored ex-slave from the South. Despite their successes in these regards, however, neither author gave the embryonic black literature the original, indigenous culture hero or the assessment of the meaning of being black in America that the renaissance needed to establish its imaginative independence

18. Frank J. Webb, *The Garies and Their Friends* (London: G. Routledge, 1857).

from conventional abolitionist literature. Martin R. Delany helped to fill this need in January, 1859, when his novel of black nationalism, *Blake; or the Huts of America*, first appeared in serial form.[19]

In Henrico Blacus, a pure black West Indian who anglicizes his name to Blake, Delany created the first black nationalistic culture hero in Afro-American literature. Blake's espousal of revolutionary politics is but one of several traits that ally him to the rebel-heroes of nineteenth-century romantic literature. "Alone and friendless, without a home, a fugitive from slavery, a child of misfortune and outcast of the world, floating on the cold surface of chance," Blake superficially resembles one of Byron's romantic aliens.[20] But unlike Manfred or Cain, Blake is tormented by social outrage, not by personal guilt—a fact that leads him to dedicate himself to freedom for the slave and nationhood for the African peoples of America. To this end he circulates clandestinely through the South, preaching a message of slave insurrection justified by a subjective reinterpretation of the Christian gospel. Spurning the religion of acquiescence and ignorance imposed on him by the whites, Blake becomes a political and moral renegade with his announcement, " 'I'll obey that [in the Bible] intended for me.' " This kind of radical intellectual individualism, which is Captain Ahab's nemesis, does not lead to Blake's downfall but rather to the inspiration of the black masses enslaved in America and Cuba. In other words, the black culture hero's desperate assertion of self does not alienate him from his people, as so often occurs with the protagonists of Melville and Hawthorne; it makes him an example to them of their corporate capacity for liberation. Thus *Blake* links romantic individualism and revolutionary politics in a manner much more akin to the

19. Martin R. Delany, *Blake; or the Huts of America* appeared serially in the *Weekly Anglo-African*, from November 26, 1861, until late May, 1862. The vagueness of the latter date is due to the fact that the final chapters of the novel have not yet been recovered. In 1859, almost all of the opening half of the novel was published in the *Anglo-African Magazine* for the first time. The version of the novel used in this essay is Floyd J. Miller's edition of the *Weekly Anglo-African* text (Boston: Beacon, 1970).

20. Delany, *Blake*, 101.

thinking of Shelley and Byron than to the writing of American romantics.

Like many of the fictional works of the American renaissance, however, *Blake*'s plot develops as a quest story. After becoming a fugitive slave early in the novel, Blake does not set out in search of freedom in the North, the typical goal of the individual quester of the fugitive-slave narrative. He chooses instead to seek a higher ideal, the spiritual enlightenment of his fellow slaves as preparation for their eventual revolt. Like many Promethean protagonists in romantic literature, Blake considers knowledge the key to liberation. After uttering his own version of "NO! in thunder" to the God of white Christianity, he takes up the metaphysical problem that dogs black protagonists from the original eighteenth-century slave narratives forward—the duty of the religious slave to the Christian God. Rejecting the old formula of earthly patience leading to a heavenly reward, Blake promulgates a black religious ethic whose cardinal tenet might be summed up in Ahab's belief that the "right worship" of a tyrant God is "defiance." Thus the part of the Bible intended for black obedience is that which enjoins holy war against the oppressors of Jehovah's people. As Blake the prophet-revolutionary says of his messianic "errand" among his people: "I am for war—war upon the whites. I come to bring deliverance to the captive and freedom to the bond." This kind of apocalyptic vision, with its basis in spiritual alienation, disillusionment with America's dream of the New Jerusalem, and a search for a sociopolitical ideal, furnishes the most compelling evidence of Delany's participation in the apocalyptic tradition of nineteenth-century American literature, to which Poe, Hawthorne, Melville, and Mark Twain made the most famous contributions.

The novelists of the first Afro-American literary renaissance, therefore, were experimentalists in their genre, because they each had a story to tell which could not fit into the narrow borders of the fugitive-slave narrative. Brown wished to survey the institution of slavery throughout the South; de facto racism in the urban North was the Philadelphia-born Webb's major interest. Through Henry Blake's travels, Delany set out across the slave states, followed a route of the Underground Railroad to Ontario, voyaged to Africa and back on a slave ship, and finally halted in Cuba, where a revolution of Africans, American blacks, and Hispanic mixed-bloods allowed him to underline his novel's internationalist theme. Through the work of these three novelists, then, the province of the black narrative writer was extended beyond the individual experience of a slave to include the sectional, national, and international dimensions of collective black experience. Moreover, the romantic novelist's prerogative enabled Brown, Webb, and Delany to transcend the facts of the slave's circumscribed reality, to which ex-slave narrators had been consigned and limited in the fugitive-slave narrative. For Brown and Webb the novel could expose areas of black American history and experience that the slave narrative had never been intended to explore. For Delany the novel offered the chance to imagine an alternative world, a Pan-African sociopolitical ideal, which the slave narrative, given its documentary realism and abolitionist politics, could neither conceive of nor countenance. In these several respects, the novelists of the 1850s broke ground necessary to the evolution of a viable twentieth-century Afro-American fiction.

The efforts of these pioneering black novelists alone could not have produced an Afro-American literary renaissance in the 1850s, however. Expansion of the writer's imaginative horizons and transcendence of the mere facts of slave experience constituted but one half of the liberating effect that the spirit of romanticism had on mid-century Afro-American authors. If a burgeoning confidence in the creative self led to the rise of the novel out of the slave narrative, then an inward-directed candor about the psychological development of the self inspired an equally important generic evolution from the slave narrative—the black American autobiography *per se*. Henry Bibb's self-authored *Narrative* (1849) anticipated this new form by replacing the figure of the indomitable, single-minded fugitive with a protagonist whose divided allegiances and interior conflicts cast the black man's struggle for freedom on a more psychologically complex plane than could be found in earlier narratives of slave heroics. Samuel

Ringgold Ward's *Autobiography of a Fugitive Negro* (1855), the unprecedented account of a black expatriate who had no first-hand experience of slavery, further pondered the nature of the Afro-American quest for selfhood. After thoroughly repudiating the myth of the free person of color in the North, Ward implied that only through alienation from America could a black person engage in unhampered self-discovery. Finally, in *My Bondage and My Freedom* (1855), Frederick Douglass gave the Afro-American renaissance its consummate narrative work, an autobiography that for the first time melded a black man's experience as a slave *and* freeman into a unified initiation pattern. Revaluating the meaning of *bondage* and *freedom* as Bibb and Ward did, Douglass rethought and rewrote his life story so that a dialectic of psychological progress appeared throughout, leading him to a liberating self- and social consciousness.

In his *Narrative*, Henry Bibb pointed the way toward new standards of psychological realism in Afro-American narratives by refusing to adopt the popular image of the heroic fugitive, the rugged black individualist who, through faith in God or steadfast will, overcomes crushing odds to seize the prize of freedom. In an unusual confessional vein, he told a story more pathetic than heroic of a man who repeatedly escapes the physical bonds of slavery, only to return to captivity again and again because of the emotional chains that bind him to his slave wife. Bibb's self-portrait reveals a man tormented by warring psychic commitments, caught up in a cycle of freedom and self-enslavement from which there seems to be no exit. In his early years, brutal treatment "kindled a fire of liberty within my breast," which "seemed a part of my nature; it was first revealed to me by the inevitable laws of nature's God."[21] These romantic promptings from intuition and nature impel the young slave toward the ideal of liberty, so that at eighteen he "pledge[s] . . . from this course never to be shaken while a single pulsation of my heart shall continue to throb for Liberty." But after dedicating himself spiritually to this ideal, Bibb succumbs to an emotional lapse: "I suffered my-

21. *Narrative of the Life and Adventures of Henry Bibb*, 17.

self to be turned aside by the fascinating charms of a female, who gradually won my attention from an object so high as that of liberty." As a result, Bibb compromises his spiritual ideal for the sake of his passion, the subsequent events of his life unfolding the bitter fruit of that compromise.

Married in 1833, Bibb chose four years later between his emotional attachments and his fundamental commitment to personal liberty, reaching freedom in Ohio in January, 1838. Yet he could not forget the ties which held him to his slave past, namely, his slave wife and daughter. Thus in 1838, 1839, and 1845 he returned to Kentucky for them, suffering recapture and reenslavement twice as a result of his efforts. His life story takes on a near-tragic fatalism as it becomes clear that he cannot have both freedom and family. Still, his sense of guilt and responsibility cannot be eased by his continued self-sacrifices and failures. Consequently Bibb's *Narrative* does not progress along the linear, ultimately comic plot sequence that was a convention of most fugitive-slave narratives, including those of Douglass and Wells Brown. Bibb pictures himself trapped in an inextricable dilemma, in which the aspirations of the spirit toward freedom pull against the obligations of the emotions toward loved ones. While his intuitive self longs for the ideal, his physical and emotional self marries Bibb to the real, in this case, slavery as represented by his wife and child. Nor can Bibb ever resolve this desperate predicament through his own willed action. Only after his wife "gives him up" and becomes her master's concubine is he able to acquit himself of his responsibility to her, though not of his guilt for fathering a child in slavery.

The conflict within the divided self of the lover-idealist is not an unfamiliar dilemma for the American hero, be he Owen Warland or Pierre Glendenning, Jay Gatsby or Quentin Compson. As his white counterparts in romantic fiction suffer, so Henry Bibb suffers from the irreconcilability of ideal prospects and the irredeemable past. In fact, in one sense Bibb's story rings the most topical chord of these American romantic tragedies, since this black quester aspires to the purest of American ideals—individual freedom—not the artistic self-realization, moral atonement, or social and economic magnificence that motivate his white counterparts. Most important to the rise of the black auto-biography, Bibb's *Narrative* discloses a dynamic inner principle at work in a black man's pursuit of freedom long after he has escaped physical enslavement. Besides shedding this new light on the deeper meanings of the black quest, the psychological conflict within Henry Bibb distinguishes him from preceding slave nar-rators, whose struggles are generally with outside forces and whose successes can usually be traced to simple origins, like con-version to Christianity or accumulated outrage toward slavery. Bibb's decision not to portray himself as a conventional fugitive hero freed him to adhere more closely to an individually deter-mined standard of self-definition as he told his story. This de-cision, in turn, previewed a redefining of the concept of heroism in terms of artistic truth to the self, which would become a bed-rock assumption of the Afro-American renaissance in the roman-tic 1850s.

To Samuel Ringgold Ward, truth to the self meant freedom to express a bitterness toward America, especially its government and professed Christianity, unparalleled in Afro-American nar-ratives up to that time. The Christian patience and forbearance of the Negro were proverbial in white wisdom, both North and South, and the fugitive slave who did not state his willingness to forgive his master was a rarity in the slave narratives of the 1830s and 1840s. For Ward, however, this masquerade of black peo-ple's true emotions was insupportable. To those whites who would accuse him of "bitterness" in his book, he replied early on, "Such persons talk as if they knew but little of human nature, and less of Negro character, else they would wonder rather that, what with slavery and Negro-hate, the mass of us are not either depressed into idiocy or excited into demons."[22] Clearly, such a remark directed at widespread white ignorance of "Negro char-acter" made Ward's revelations and justifications of outrage and bitterness in himself another kind of "NO! in thunder" necessary to the creative independence of the new black literature. A total

22. Samuel Ringgold Ward, *Autobiography of a Fugitive Negro* (London: John Snow, 1855), 28–29.

iconoclast, Ward used his story to repudiate his connection with the American people: "Nowhere in the world has the Negro so bitter, so relentless enemies, as are the Americans"; the United States as a nation is "that worst of all countries"; and Christianity within its borders is "more corrupt than even its politics." Such a demonstration of intellectual audacity showed that the new black renaissance, even more than its white counterpart, would not be hemmed in by what was considered decorous, politic, treasonous, or sacred by the mainstream American audience.

From the standpoint of the storytelling art, *Autobiography of a Fugitive Negro* did not make a substantial contribution to the evolution of the Afro-American narrative as a literary form. Ward's story was unique in black letters at that time, for he had been taken from slavery at age three by his fugitive parents and raised in poverty in New York City, free from the threat of return to slavery. Unfortunately, the author covers the entirety of his childhood and adolescence in only three pages and employs a loose narrative structure throughout the remainder of the volume, wherein he describes his "Anti-Slavery Labours" in the United States, Canada, and England. The account of Ward's early ministerial career and antislavery activism, culminating in his indictment for allegedly aiding a fugitive slave's escape from federal marshalls in 1851, is dramatically rendered through a series of disillusioning experiences that radicalize Ward and make fugitiveship his only choice. But the latter half of the book, on Ward's years in Canada and Britain, follows an episodic pattern interspersed with accounts of abolition meetings, sketches of the famous and near-famous, travel notes, and observations and asides on a wide range of race-related topics. The author takes leave of the reader after proving himself a success on the lecture platform of England and in the company of the most influential and respectable people of the realm, who receive him as "an equal brother man." This sort of comic conclusion, in which freedom is finally attained, though ironically in a monarchy not a democracy, was used in a number of fugitive-slave narratives published before and after Ward's *Autobiography*.[23] Ending his

23. See *Narrative of the Adventures and Escape of Moses Roper*, the

story this way resolved Ward's lonely quest conventionally and rather patly, while it skirted the crucial issue that remained before the writers of the black renaissance. Could the Afro-American still discover and develop himself according to his own ideals while living in racist America in the middle of the nineteenth century?

The example of Frederick Douglass in *My Bondage and My Freedom* suggested that this question could be answered with a qualified yes, but only if the Afro-American realized that the struggle begun in the South for independence and self-determination continued unabated in the North, especially among the professed "friends" of the black man. Douglass was not the first freeman to update his original narrative with "revised and expanded" editions of his continuing story. But he was the first to consider a new installment of his autobiography an occasion for a wholesale reassessment of the pattern and progress of his life from twenty-one years of slavery through seventeen years of "freedom." His *Narrative*, appearing ten years before *My Bondage and My Freedom*, treated his life in freedom in the cursory and largely optimistic way of the standard fugitive-slave narrative. A mere 7 percent of the *Narrative* is devoted to Douglass' free years, and except for one early instance of job discrimination (which a Douglass footnote says had since been rectified by abolitionist effort), life in the North is pictured in rosy terms for the fugitive. Under the protection of abolitionists, he becomes a self-supporting member of a prosperous and self-respecting black working class. He receives intellectual sustenance through the *Liberator* of William Lloyd Garrison and finds an avenue for free self-expression on the antislavery platform. All these happy turns of events fulfill Douglass' American Dream and leave the

---

Narrative of Henry Watson, A Fugitive Slave (Boston: Bela Marsh, 1848), William Craft's *Running A Thousand Miles for Freedom; or The Escape of William and Ellen Craft from Slavery* (London: William Tweedie, 1860), and Francis Fedric's *Slave Life in Virginia and Kentucky* (London: Wertheim, Macintosh, and Hunt, 1863). The number of references to English publishers in these footnotes discloses an irony of the Afro-American renaissance—that its flowering depended much more on the goodwill of the British press than on the American.

reader with a feeling of virtue and pluck rewarded and a case of cruel injustice satisfyingly closed.

The conclusion of *My Bondage and My Freedom* seeks neither to vindicate the American Dream nor to reassure the liberal American reader of the mid-nineteenth century. The book traces an initiation into northern racism that Douglass had chosen not to mention in his *Narrative*, and a pattern of disillusionment and growing self-reliance that Douglass probably did not see unfolding when he wrote his *Narrative*. For instance, a major eye-opening experience for Douglass in the North came in the first year of his freedom when he applied for membership in a Methodist church in New Bedford, Massachusetts. Learning that he would not be seated in the congregation because of his color, Douglass at first accepted this on the assumption that it was a concession to the prejudices of unconverted visitors to the church. But when he was refused equal access to communion at a time when only church members were present, Douglass became aware of the true reasons for segregation in the church. As a result he left and joined a black Methodist body. Not a single allusion to this incident or to this kind of institutionalized racism is allowed to darken the sunny conclusion of the *Narrative*, though the time of the incident—the winter of 1838–39—was well within the purview of that book. On the other hand, the entire episode is recounted in detail in *My Bondage and My Freedom* as a means of illustrating the author's initial ignorance and naïveté about racism in the North.

In *My Bondage and My Freedom* Douglass chose to plot his life as a freeman according to a dialectic that arises out of his initial faith in, and eventual disillusionment with, many of the supposed ideals and idealists of the North. His quest for the American Dream does not end with this disillusionment, nor does he reject the dream for the hope of freedom abroad, as did Ward. Instead, Douglass learns to withdraw his allegiance from white authorities and award it to the self-willed guide within that had inspired him to resist more overt forms of repression when he was a slave in the South. As a result, a pattern of misplaced faith, disillusionment, and subsequent self-reliance emerges throughout the "Freedom" section of *My Bondage and My Freedom*. While evident in Douglass' religious experience among the ostensibly liberal Methodists of New Bedford, the pattern provides, more importantly, an explanation for the development of his singular political career from Garrisonian subaltern to independent black spokesman.

Both versions of Douglass' autobiography agree that he joined the Garrisonian antislavery crusade with unqualified admiration for its leader and his methods and goals. *My Bondage and My Freedom* states that, fresh from slavery, Douglass placed the *Liberator* "next to the bible" and considered Garrison himself "the Moses, raised up by God, to deliver his modern Israel from bondage." In 1855 Douglass could see what he did not recognize in 1845—that as a young man he was "something of a hero worshiper" and that he joined the antislavery movement "in the full gush of unsuspecting enthusiasm." Like a too-credulous religious zealot, the ex-slave gave himself totally to the "holy cause," believing in its gospel of racial brotherhood in Christ and universal emancipation. "For a time I was made to forget that my skin was dark and my hair crisped. . . . I soon, however, found that my enthusiasm had been extravagant; that hardships and dangers were not passed; and that the life now before me, had shadows as well as sunbeams."[24]

The "shadows" dominate the last forty pages of *My Bondage and My Freedom*. Beginning with the anecdote of the condescending abolitionists who assigned him the facts while reserving the philosophy for themselves, Douglass scores a series of humiliations, threats, and subtle pressures against his self-development in the North. Segregation and public defamation infringe on his physical freedom, but more disturbing are the revelations of discriminatory and authoritarian attitudes among the abolitionists with whom he must deal. It is they who try to confine his public speaking to the simple facts of his slave life, they who urge him not to purchase his freedom when he has the chance, they who oppose his plans to undertake a new career as an editor and

24. Douglass, *My Bondage and My Freedom*, 360.

journalist in 1848. By the time of the writing of *My Bondage and My Freedom*, Douglass understands the pattern of his past well enough to conclude, "I am not sure that I was not under the influence of something like a slavish adoration of my Boston friends." Thus he realizes that the climax of his life lay in his decision to break with Garrisonian abolitionist policy, to renounce his "discipleship" and accept "the common punishment of apostates." Knowing that "the abolitionists themselves were not entirely free from" the "prejudice against color" pervading America, Douglass can no longer follow with blind faith their "Messiah" or their "holy cause." Chastened and more skeptical, the lone writer-journalist sets out on a new phase of life at the end of *My Bondage and My Freedom*, dependent only on his private apprehension of the truth and dedicated only to the advancement of the black community. As editor of his own paper, not a speaker for another's program, Douglass redefines his mission to emphasize his new community orientation. The "best means of emancipation" is "to promote the moral, social, religious, and intellectual elevation of the free colored people." "Progress," Douglass concludes, "is yet possible"; his story of self-realization and ultimate identification with the black community proves it.

My Bondage and My Freedom epitomizes the intellectual courage, self-investigation, and social insight that are the hallmarks of the first Afro-American renaissance. The consummate autobiographical narrative of the renaissance, it joins the most outspoken fictional narrative, *Blake; or the Huts of America*, in delineating for the first time an indigenous Afro-American initiation myth. Both books trace a process by which an enslaved black man first discovers himself as an individual through resistance to white oppression and later identifies himself as part of a community through an awareness of his continuing social isolation in America. Henry Blake becomes an heroic fugitive after denouncing oppressive southern religion and converting to a kind of revolutionary Christianity. However, Delany could resolve Blake's alien status in America only by removing him from this country and making him the leader of a militant black nationalist movement. Neither the facts of Douglass' life nor his political convictions would let him imagine such an outcome for his own career. He had to render the process of Afro-American initiation within a lifelong context of repression and struggle in the United States.

As Douglass pictured it, the black man's struggle against oppression was fought on much the same psychological and spiritual terrain whether he found himself a literal slave in the South or declassed and powerless in the North. The climax of Douglass' life as a slave does not occur when he escapes but rather when he resists the authority of a white man, Edward Covey, whose role it is to discipline him and "break him" to the proper manner of a slave. Similarly, the high point of Douglass' free years is marked by another act of resistance to white authority, namely, the authority of Garrison and other white abolitionists, whose discipline is milder than Covey's but just as inhibitive of the black man's growth in independence. In the South, Douglass informs his reader, blacks are "trained from the cradle up, to think and feel that their masters are superior, and invested with a sort of sacredness." In the North, Douglass shows his reader how he had endowed Garrison with this sort of "sacredness," and his "Boston friends" in general with a "slavish adoration." To free himself from such "masters" and their quasi-religious authority over him, the black man must renounce his faith in them even though this seems an act fraught with impiety and the likelihood of damnation. Thus, before the fight with Covey, Douglass says, "My religious views on the subject of resisting my master, had suffered a serious shock . . . and my hands were no longer tied by my religion. . . . I had now to this extent 'backslidden' from this point in the slave's religious creed." His resistance to Covey manifests his new "fallen state." As a freeman, Douglass once again backslides, this time from Garrison's "holy cause," with the result that his "ambitious" and "presumptuous" act (in the eyes of the Garrisonians) incurs "the common punishment of apostates." However, to be damned and cast out of white men's favor is not the black man's tragedy but a prelude to his salvation, as Douglass' slave and free experiences further attest. Relocated at a new plantation after his stint with Covey, Douglass immediately starts a Sunday school to share with his fellow slaves his realization of "the advantages of intelligence over ignorance." This experiment in community leaves Douglass with more satisfaction than any other work he has participated in before or since. With his "brother slaves" he feels part of a unit in which there is "no elevating one at the expense of the other." Running away for his personal freedom, therefore, was "intensely grievous" to Douglass because it separated him from the black community and soon thrust him into a white community in which he discovers a great deal of racist "elevating one at the expense of the other." In the conclusion of *My Bondage and My Freedom*, however, Douglass intends to reestablish his ties to the black community through his newspaper, a decision that bodes well for him both as an individualist-leader and as a very socially oriented man.

Like Douglass, each of the major writers of the first Afro-American renaissance proved himself to be individualistic and self-conscious, but community-affirming as well. While these literary pioneers wrote out of a determination to open their own intercourse with the white world, they also had in mind a creative demonstration of the power of blackness within themselves and the untapped black community. In one sense, the power they hoped to unleash was that which would eventually bring an end to slavery. But they also wished to empower their embryonic black audience with a vision of its corporate capacities. The parting promise of *My Bondage and My Freedom*—that "progress is possible"—bespeaks therefore either the explicit message or the underlying motive of all the black renaissance writing of the 1850s. Because of the romantic vision of this renaissance, the Afro-American autobiography and *Bildungsroman* was grounded in a sustaining cultural tradition that sees self-discovery and self-expression leading to a nurturing community identification and ultimately a hopeful conclusion to the black quest in America.

Thomas Wolfe
and the Place
He Came From

❧

LOUIS D. RUBIN, JR.

Thomas Wolfe and the South was the subject of the first essay
on southern literature I published, almost a quarter-century ago.
In that essay I went about demonstrating, or attempting to demonstrate, that Wolfe was indubitably a southern writer, as if that
were of itself a kind of badge of literary honor; and to prove it I
drew up a list of characteristics customarily ascribed to southern
writers and tried to show how each applied to Wolfe's writing.
These included such things as the fondness for rhetoric, the sense
of place, the storytelling quality and the sense of the family that
is supposed to go along with it, the consciousness of the past and
of time, the sense of evil, and so forth. I came to dislike that
essay very much, and the next time I had occasion to revise and
augment the set of essays on contemporary southern literature in
which it appeared, I scrapped it and got my friend and Chapel
Hill colleague C. Hugh Holman to write one instead. He did
so, and more to my satisfaction. My early essay, however, remains available; every so often somebody discovers it, and I am
always embarrassed to see it quoted. I have not wavered at all
in my conviction that Wolfe is a southern writer, but I don't
think that lining up a set of the official characteristics of southern
literature and then trying to show that Wolfe fits them and so is
eligible for the prized blue ribbon—or should I say blue-and-
gray ribbon—is very helpful in understanding either Wolfe or
southern literature. It is something like trying to prove that a
great batter like Ted Williams was a good baseball player because he knew how to play line drives off the left field wall in
Fenway Park.

61

Wolfe isn't a southern writer because he sometimes wrote like William Faulkner or Robert Penn Warren, but because most of the time he wrote like Thomas Wolfe. And if a writer as good as Wolfe was at his best doesn't fit the official list of characteristics of southern writing, then what should be suspect is not Wolfe but the list. What I tried to do, I am afraid, both in that earlier essay and in part in the book I published on Wolfe several years later, was to make Wolfe into an honorary member of the Nashville Agrarians, which strikes me now as a pretty gratuitous enterprise. Wolfe did what he had to do, and they did what they had to do, and what is nice is that we have both.

On the other hand, it is instructive to recall why it seemed a good idea to try to show, back in 1953, that Thomas Wolfe was beyond question a southern writer. This was the time when the Southern Literary Renascence that began after the First World War was just beginning to be identified as an important phenomenon in American literary history—until then it had been thought of primarily as a fortuitous assortment of good books. The book for which my essay was written was the first full-fledged examination of the overall achievement of modern southern literature. William Faulkner, after years of toiling in something resembling critical obscurity, was only just beginning to be recognized as perhaps the premier writer of fiction of our century, and the excitement of this discovery was widespread. On the other hand, the southern poet-critics—Ransom, Tate, Warren, Brooks—were at the height of their authority, and what they said was so about literature meant a great deal (and still does to me).

We had recently been through a depression, a new deal, and a world war. Each of these phenomena had involved a great deal of ideological paraphernalia, and as is always the way, literature had been placed in their service. In the 1930s it was the Marxist, proletarian novel. In the 1940s it was the novel of involvement. We had gone through a long period of trying to make out that books such as *The Grapes of Wrath, U.S.A., For Whom the Bell Tolls, A Bell for Adano, Studs Lonigan, Strange Fruit,* and so on were the principal achievements of modern American literature.

We were a little tired of it; we wanted to learn how to read fiction and poetry again *as* fiction and poetry, for their formal literary excellence, and not as ideological documents. So the novelists such as Faulkner and Warren and Porter and other southerners, and the poets such as Tate, Ransom, and Warren, who had never lost sight of that fact and had generally refused to take part as novelists and poets in the various popular causes, were now being discovered or rediscovered with delight. These were, as a scholar-friend of mine once wrote, the southern years, and the traditional southern literary virtues of formal excellence and moral relevance, having been revitalized and given great imaginative energy as the literary South had moved into the modern world, now seemed very attractive indeed. There was also the additional advantage that the literary marketplace in New York had run out of ideological gimmicks, now that literary proletarianism and literary patriotism had run their course, so it couldn't put up much of a fight against literature as literature, however unsalable and superficially unexciting mere literary excellence might be. So until the civil rights movement got going in the late 1950s and New York had a good excuse for dealing with literature (some of it very good literature indeed) as ideology once again, the rich formal achievement of the best southern literature was permitted to be read and admired, as generally it wasn't before and hasn't been since.

For these reasons and others, then, the period of the late 1940s and early 1950s was a time when merely being a good southern writer seemed to be a gesture in the direction of literary distinction, and there was widespread and deserved appreciation of the best southern writing of our time.

The trouble was, however, that with any such consensus of taste, no matter how good, there always goes along a kind of orthodoxy. Virtues are soon codified; the approaches and techniques that are, for good writers, the creative means for the act of discovery that is literature are made into the ends themselves. Because some southern authors (*e.g.*, Faulkner and Tate) went at the art of literature in certain creative ways, and because those ways had clearly worked and filled certain genuine artistic needs, it followed that that was the southern way to do it, and any writer who didn't do it that way was inferior and not a true southern literary man. Thus, because Wolfe didn't write fiction the way Faulkner wrote fiction, Wolfe was neither as important nor as "southern" a novelist as Faulkner.

Now I happen to believe that Wolfe *isn't* as important a writer as Faulkner, but the reason he isn't is not that he didn't write his books the way that Faulkner wrote his; it's because Faulkner wrote a different kind of novel better than Wolfe wrote his kind. And conversely, if Wolfe *is* an important novelist, as I certainly believe he is, the reasons why he is might well have nothing to do with resembling Faulkner.

Perhaps that seems obvious—certainly it is trite enough to be obvious—but it isn't the way literary movements and schools and groups tend to approach things. We tend to erect our characteristic methods, techniques, and attitudes into orthodoxies. We make the highly creative techniques of some writers into legalisms that impede our own imaginative response to other writers. One writer's method is another's impoverishment; one writer's need is another's inhibition.

Well and good. But what if one is so struck with the imaginative achievement of one group of writers and finds so much that is good and stimulating in the way they approach their craft and at the same time one is also powerfully drawn to another and different kind of writer, whom those writers and many critics generally don't like (and also don't always understand)? What does one do? I expect that one attempts to do what I think I tried to do with Thomas Wolfe: to take the insights and apparatus and attitudes that fit the one group and try to demonstrate—both to oneself and to others whom one likes and admires—that the writer in question has been misread and really isn't so different and is a good writer *because* at bottom he is really doing the same things that the others are. Thus Thomas Wolfe is an important southern writer, not because of Thomas Wolfe's own unique version of the human experience in southern guise, but because he resembles other important southern writers. Which is a pretty silly business.

Now the American South is a large and complex region, with some vastly different subregions within it, and the literature it has produced partakes of these divisions—Hugh Holman has identified these as the Tidewater, the Piedmont, and the Deep South. He has selected Ellen Glasgow as exemplar of the Tidewater sensibility in literature, Wolfe for the Piedmont, and Faulkner for the Deep South. But if you are not careful, you tend to think of the South exclusively in terms of one of these subregions and to say that the writing characteristic of the particular subregion is southern literature and anything else isn't southern literature.

It is also true that the sense of community was so strong throughout the South, and still in many ways remains so, that to say one is a southerner is not merely a description but an act of community identification. "In Dixie Land I'll take my stand." To be a southerner has meant to *belong* to a club, as it were, or perhaps a fraternity, a cult, a society, with some social prestige attached to the membership. In William Faulkner's novel *Absalom, Absalom!*, when Quentin Compson is told by a Canadian that he can't understand why southerners feel the way they do, Quentin tells him, "You can't understand it. You would have to be born there." I have seen that remark excoriated by some critics as snobbish, undemocratic, pretentious—but none of the critics who object to it is a southerner. Well, there *is* a certain amount of cliquishness attached to it; to an extent it is not just Quentin explaining, but his creator bragging a bit. Whether he had any right to feel privileged or whether anyone has such a right, because of being a southerner, is another matter; the fact is that many have felt that way, and still do, and that among them have been William Faulkner and also Thomas Wolfe.

Yet in certain ways Wolfe didn't appear to belong to the club. For part of this self-conscious identification as a southerner had, perhaps even still has, a certain amount of social overtone, as well as literary and critical assumptions, and in a kind of complex but not clearly defined way there was a relationship between the two. Most of the important southern writers of the 1920s, 1930s, and 1940s were of the gentry, or perhaps the upper middle class would be a better way of describing it; in any event, "of good family" as the expression went (which as I think Ellen Glasgow once pointed out was to say something very different from they were "of good people"—*i.e.*, of the rural working or lower middle class, the so-called "yeomanry."). The southern writers weren't aristocrats, mind you, and none grew up in stately Tidewater mansions. But the "Big House" and the southern gentlemen were involved in the southern ideal, and almost every one of the twentieth-century southern writers has at one point in his or her work (often at frequent points) presented, with more than a little approval, characters who look down disdainfully upon the "trash" and the "riff-raff" without "family"—*i.e.*, without approved social connections.

But Thomas Wolfe made a *point* of his working-class lineage. He wrote an autobiographical novel about growing up in a boardinghouse. He was actively hostile to and critical of southern aristocratic pretense, and he liked to boast that his background was working class, yeomanry. Now it would have been all right if he had simply accepted the fact; but to boast of it, and furthermore to suggest, as he sometimes did, that because of his origins *he* was honest and open and democratic and genuine, while those who weren't from similar origins were snobbish and defensive and aristocratic and full of pretense, was another matter entirely.

This was not merely a matter of subject matter or of authorial biography. It also, and more importantly perhaps, involved ideas about literary technique and attitude. The literary virtues of the best southern writing—formal elegance, a reverence for tradition, restraint, self-sufficiency—were, in an important way I believe, those customarily ascribed to the aristocracy. And the two tended to get all involved with each other, in a fashion that was not logical perhaps but was nonetheless pervasive.

Let me offer two quotations from the critical writings of Allen Tate (the man whom, I might add, I happen to admire most among all twentieth-century authors). In one, dated 1931, Tate was writing about poetry: "A mind without moral philosophy is incapable of understanding poetry. For poetry, of all the arts, demands a serenity of view and a settled temper of the mind, and most of all the power to detach one's own needs from the experience set forth in the poem. A moral sense so organized sets limits to human nature, and is content to observe them." In the other, dated 1936, Tate was writing about the Old South: "Antebellum man, insofar as he achieved a unity between his moral nature and his livelihood, was a traditional man. He dominated the means of life; he was not dominated by it. I think that the distinguishing feature of a traditional society is simply that. In order to make a livelihood men do not have to put aside their moral natures." The terms in the two passages are almost interchangeable; the same sense of restraint, of classical wholeness, of unified personality that characterizes the gentleman of the Old South is used to characterize the writing of poetry. Tate, to be sure, wasn't confusing the two realms, but many people did.

Such terms clearly didn't fit the work of Thomas Wolfe. His was no serenity of view, and his temper of mind was not settled but highly volatile and excitable. The idea of a harmonious unity of personality, dominating every facet of its experience, acting unconsciously and classically out of a completely traditional and accepted set of responses to experience, was the last way one might think to describe how Wolfe went about either living his life or writing his books. He was highly and voraciously romantic; he wanted to storm the gates of Heaven, and never mind the consequences. Restraint? Why, he poured the language on at all times, held back not at all. And as for detaching his own needs from the experience set forth in his books, it is obvious that no more literally autobiographical and nakedly personal a writer than Thomas Wolfe ever lived.

What I am suggesting is that those literary characteristics which were most valued by most of the southern writers of the 1920s and 1930s, and which in many ways exemplify the best features of much of their art, were also seen as socially characteristic of an aristocratic ideal—and there was the implication, though nobody ever came right out and said it, that the creator of Eugene Gant, though born in a state of the former Confederacy, was from the wrong side of the tracks and wrote like it. Mind you, the best of the other southern writers didn't think of it that way at all, as far as I know; but a good many lesser authorities who wrote about southern letters suggested as much.

I recall, for example, approaching an American literature scholar of some reputation, who liked very much to think of himself as a southern gentleman, and asking him to direct a dissertation I wanted to write on Thomas Wolfe as a southern writer. His response was that he didn't think of Wolfe as being a southern writer; he thought that in spirit Wolfe belonged among the midwestern writers. So I had to look elsewhere (and finally found a Frenchman who was willing to help me). Ostensibly the man was making a literary distinction—*i.e.*, that Wolfe's work could be best understood when viewed alongside such writers as Dreiser, Lewis, Anderson, Sandburg, and so forth, rather than alongside Faulkner and Warren and the other southerners. But he was also expressing, conscious of it or not, a social judgment; he was telling me that as a writer Wolfe was not a gentleman.

For like many other readers, this scholar had formed his notion of what a southern author should be from the local color and genteel literature of the late nineteenth and early twentieth centuries, and when the newer writers came along, once the shock of their being different was blunted, he had somehow managed to fit them into the same social milieu. The perspective from which the literature was ostensibly to be viewed and supposedly had been written was that of the gentleman. Since Thomas Wolfe wasn't a southern gentleman and had few of the virtues, either literary or social, customarily ascribed to southern gentlemen, it was quite clear that Wolfe wasn't a southern writer!

Consider another illustration of the same kind of bias, this time from, of all persons, Herbert Marshall McLuhan. (Few people recall that back in the old days, before Marshall McLuhan discovered mediums and messages, he was a mere literary critic.) Here are several sentences from his essay on "The Southern Quality": "The impersonal formal code which permits a formal expression of inward emotion makes it pointless for people to interpret one another constantly, as they do in most 'realistic' novels. There is thus in the Southern novel a vacuum where we might expect introspection. (It is quite pronounced even in *Huck Fin.*) The stress falls entirely on slight human gestures, external events which are obliquely slanted to flash light or shade on character."

The image—and McLuhan was quite aware of it—is of the gentleman, reserved, formal, punctilious, who is never so vulgar as to attempt to penetrate beyond the formal, arm's-length social ambience. McLuhan then goes on to point out that Thomas Wolfe partook of this impulse, too, but in his case the result was to leave him "locked up in his own passionate solitude." Wolfe, he continues, "has all the passion without any of the formal means of constraint and communication which make it tolerable. He was a Southerner by attitude but not by tradition."

The implied social judgment is obvious. Wolfe was not a gentleman, so didn't know the inherited rules of gentlemanly conduct, but since he was a southerner by birth, he couldn't help but have absorbed the proper attitude from his betters! Now what bosh and balderdash, as they say. The idea of the southern novel not permitting characters to interpret each other leaves out such episodes as Thomas Sutpen talking to General Compson and Miss Rosa Coldfield talking to Quentin Compson and Quentin Compson talking to Shreve McCannon in Faulkner's *Absalom, Absalom!* It leaves out Lacy Buchan's whole method of narration in Tate's *The Fathers*. It leaves out Jack Burden on the subject of Willie Stark in *All The King's Men*. It leaves out Eudora Welty's *The Optimist's Daughter*. It leaves out—but a better way to get at the appropriateness of that particular pronouncement might be to say what it includes. It includes, so far as I can tell, Stark Young and Thomas Nelson Page, and not a great deal else.

Why such a pronouncement from a critic with as much intelligence as Marshall McLuhan? It was simply that McLuhan confused the subject matter of some southern fiction with its techniques—captivated with what Allen Tate, John Ransom, and others have written, often admiringly, *about* the southern gentleman, he moved insensibly to assuming that Tate, for example, wrote *as* a southern gentleman, which is precisely what Tate often went to demonstrate was quite impossible to do if one was a modern writer with anything important to say. That, Tate said, was why Poe had once been more or less driven out of Richmond, and why the good writers of his own generation had extreme difficulty in making a living while resident in the South. But such is the thematic pervasiveness of the gentlemanly ideal that it also hooked Marshall McLuhan into making numerous absurd statements, such as: "Even the characters of Erskine Caldwell are free at least from self-pity." And that statement is made about *Jeeter Lester!*

But I digress. What I have been attempting to do is to show what some of the problems are in discussing the question of Thomas Wolfe and the South. We all have our Souths, to which in varying degree we are drawn. We also have the example of some very powerful and very persuasive authors and critics who had definite ideas of what the South was and should be, and who can have a very formative and even controlling influence upon our own ways of thinking about the South and its writers, and some of their ideas are very much intertwined with their social attitudes. Yet no matter how much we may admire and value such insights, we must finally judge for ourselves in matters that concern us.

Very well, what of Thomas Wolfe and the South? *Is* Wolfe a southern writer, or merely a writer born in the South but not of it, so far as his imagination and way of writing go?

I want now to quote a fairly well-known passage from *Look Homeward, Angel*, describing Eugene Gant in his eleventh or twelfth year.

> His feeling for the South was not so much historic as it was of the core and desire of dark romanticism—that unlimited and inexplicable drunkenness, the magnetism of some men's blood that takes them into the heart of the heat, and beyond that, into the polar and emerald cold of the South as swiftly as it took the heart of the incomparable romanticist who wrote *The Rime of the Ancient Mariner*, beyond which there is nothing. And this desire of his was unquestionably enhanced by all he had read and visioned, by the romantic halo that his school history cast over

the section, by the whole fantastic distortion of that period where people were said to live in "mansions," and slavery was a benevolent institution, conducted to a constant banjo-strumming, the strewn largesses of the colonel and the shuffle-dance of his happy dependents, where all women were pure, gentle, and beautiful, all men chivalrous and brave, and the Rebel horde a company of swaggering, death-mocking cavaliers. Years later, when he could no longer think of the barren spiritual wilderness, the hostile and murderous intrenchment against all new life—when their cheap mythology, their legend of the charm of their manner, the aristocratic culture of their lives, the quaint sweetness of their drawl, made him writhe—when he could think of no return to their life and its swarming superstition without weariness and horror, so great was his fear of the legend, his fear of their antagonism, that he still pretended the most fanatic devotion to them, excusing his Northern residence on grounds of necessity rather than desire.

Finally, it occurred to him that these people had given him nothing, that neither their love nor their hatred could injure him, that he owed them nothing, and he determined that he would say so, and repay their insolence with a curse. And he did.

This passage has been cited to illustrate Wolfe's lack of relationship to the South. It is certainly a passage of repudiation. It rejects southern history, southern aristocratic pretense, southern manners, southern speech, southern womanhood, southern clannishness, southern notions of chivalry, southern culture; it describes southern life as a "barren spiritual wilderness," and it asserts that Eugene Gant eventually learned to recognize his superiority to what he had been taught to revere as southern, so that he had vowed to "repay their insolence with a curse," which, of course, was not only the passage itself but *Look Homeward, Angel* as a whole. The passage thus makes the direct autobiographical association between Thomas Wolfe's protagonist and the author himself, and is clearly intended to so do.

Now there is a passage somewhat reminiscent of that in William Faulkner's *Absalom, Absalom!* After Quentin Compson and Shreve McCannon have unraveled the long story of Thomas Sutpen and his descendants, Shreve asks Quentin why he hates the South, and Quentin replies "at once, immediately" that he doesn't hate it, repeating the statement a half-dozen times or so. Beyond doubt we are meant to see that Quentin does hate the South, and also loves it, and that love-hate relationship *is* the South for him—*is* Quentin.

But in Eugene Gant's instance there is no equivocation. He does hate it, all of it, and he wants to make it perfectly clear. He hates it because of what it did to him, and because of the hold it had for so long kept on him, and now he has told it off for good, repaid its "insolence with a curse."

Well, *is* that what he did? Not if *Look Homeward, Angel* is any indication. Along with considerable satire and savaging, there is also tremendous affection and admiration, passages of great delight with the people and places he knew in Asheville and elsewhere, passionate affirmations of its beauty, episode after episode infused with the creative joy of recollected memory, recreated experience. If one were to take all of the passages in the Wolfe fiction which attack the South and put them against all the passages which portray it, and his relation to it, in generally admiring fashion, I think they would just about balance out. In other words, there is every bit as much a love-hate relationship involved with Eugene Gant and Thomas Wolfe as with Quentin Compson and William Faulkner.

Wolfe in the passage quoted castigates the distortion of the southern plantation myth, the phony glamour of the legend of the Confederacy. He also wrote the story entitled "Chickamauga," however, and those descriptions of Lee's army en route to Gettysburg; and more importantly, he took his own particular family's history, the Westalls and Pattons who settled in the mountains of North Carolina, and the history of his father's people as well, and he did what almost every southern author of his generation did: portrayed his protagonists as the inheritors of a specific and tangible history, deeply marked and shaped by the past, and very much the creatures of the forces that placed them where they were and at the time in which they found themselves living.

Not only does the author of that passage concern himself with history and take it seriously enough to want to rectify it, but there is an important sense in which that passage *is* southern history. For what it exemplifies is the process of dislodgment, of the breaking up of the old closely knit southern premodern community before the forces of change. Wolfe describes Eugene Gant as having been born into and still very much molded by the older community, with its own history and mythology and its clearly defined social stratifications. He points out that even after he left it, he was for a long while so influenced by its pieties and its imaginative hold upon him that he pretended to a continuing allegiance. Then he says that finally he realized he was free, no longer bound and obligated, and his response was "to repay their insolence with a curse." Obviously he isn't nearly as free as he imagines, for if he were, there would be no need for so impassioned a denunciation. Wolfe is really in the position, as that paragraph amply demonstrates, of the two Quentin Compsons in *Absalom, Absalom!*—the Quentin who would live in the twentieth century and the Quentin who because he was of his time and place was still bound to the old ghost times, as Faulkner puts it. And just as Miss Rosa Coldfield suggested that Quentin might someday want to do, Wolfe has written a book about it. Surely this is precisely the cultural situation of the twentieth-century southern writer as elucidated by Allen Tate and many others: "With the war of 1914–1918, the South reentered the world— but gave a backward glance as it stepped over the border; that backward glance gave us the Southern renascence, a literature conscious of the past in the present."

But there is something more basically southern involved in the passage, even. To see it fully, we must put the episode in context. It occurs as Wolfe is describing Eliza Gant's yearly winter journeys into the South, to such places as Florida and Arkansas, for reasons of health and business. Wolfe tells how Eliza went South because of her innate suspicion of northerners—a feeling, he says, involving "fear, distrust, alienation"—and how Eugene was always taken along, "into the South, the South that burned like Dark Helen in Eugene's blood." He then proceeds to inform us of the "core and desire of dark romanticism—that unlimited and inexplicable drunkenness, the magnetism of some men's blood" that characterizes his feeling for the South.

Does this feeling evaporate when he grows older and learns to regard its mythology and its society as cheap, tawdry, oppressive? I would say that it does not, and not merely because of the evidence of so much of his work, but also because of the quality of the passage of explanation and repudiation itself. For clearly Wolfe is not describing merely a geographical section, or a set of objective environmental factors. When he depicts the South as "burning" like "Dark Helen" in his protagonist's blood, he is talking about a state of consciousness, a passionate emotional response, an entity of the spirit not to be discussed merely as quantity or as economic or sociological data. He portrays it in feminine terms, and though the South may not be "the proud Lady with the heart of fire" described in John Ransom's poem, she is a prideful woman even so; and if he has ultimately fallen out of love with her as he says, she still makes his blood run hot and he feels it necessary to tell her off in quite passionate terms. "And he did." To me, that dimension alone is enough to counter any arguments about the alleged absence of a "southern" relationship in Wolfe's work.

I recall something that Robert Penn Warren wrote in connection with Faulkner. "It is clear that Faulkner, though he gives a scrupulously faithful report of the real world, is 'mythic' . . . he is dramatizing clashes of value in a root way." Wolfe's South—more importantly, Wolfe's relationship to it—may involve a great deal of realistic description, but the affair goes beyond reportage or realistic experience, because it is powerfully caught up in feeling and emotion and in values of truth and goodness. When Auden wrote of Yeats that "mad Ireland hurt you into poetry," he was saying something that could as readily be declared of Wolfe and, for that matter, of all his southern contemporaries. And like that of his contemporaries, Wolfe's response was not only to a set of specific acts and topical problems; it was to a moral entity, one that had to be dealt with accordingly. Not only was there no room for neutrality, but the involvement involved the constant and often agonizing need to define his own moral identity in terms of the relationship to the time and place. Wolfe saw places as suffused with moral qualities, and he saw his South, above all other regions, in terms of place. "And suddenly Eugene was back in space and color and in Time," he writes in describing his own return to North Carolina, "the weather of his youth was round him, he was home again." This is not only a description of his feelings about reality; it is an accurate judgment of his fiction, which most often is surest, most firm, most vivid and least empty and forced, when it is grounded in "the South that burned like Dark Helen" in Eugene Gant's blood. It is exemplary of what Eudora Welty has written, that "it seems plain that the art that speaks most clearly, explicitly, directly, and passionately from its place of origin will remain the longest understood. It is through place that we put out roots, wherever birth, chance, fate, or our traveling selves set us down." And that place, for Wolfe, was his South—North Carolina, not merely as locale but as passionate realm of moral decision.

It is such imaginative dimensions as these and not the little descriptive motifs that I once used to "prove" a point that, presented in that way, was not worth proving, that constitute Wolfe's southern sensibility. Of course he has the addiction to rhetoric, and he uses time thematically, and he has the famous regional storytelling sense, and he is concerned with evil, and he has much to say about death, and he has the passion for detail and not much skill at abstraction. But these are only the trappings of his art, and do not of themselves help account for its distinctiveness; they would apply equally well to the fiction of, say, Edna Ferber or the late Harry Stillwell Edwards. It is the passionate moral involvement in a time and place that lies beneath these, and gives them character and form, that constitutes Thomas Wolfe's relationship with the South.

We confront the fact, however, that there does exist an important element in Wolfe's fiction which is notably different from almost every other southern author of Wolfe's day. The passage about Eugene Gant and the South certainly exemplifies it. In that passage, Wolfe is not simply telling about a character named Eugene Gant and how his feelings toward the South changed; he *is* Eugene Gant, or more properly Eugene is Thomas Wolfe, and he wants the reader to know it. In that passage he comes very close to telling us that Eugene wrote the book we are reading, and what was at least part of his motivation for so doing. This is "autobiographical fiction"—which is a way of saying that not only does the material come pretty closely and directly out of the author's experience, but that we are compelled to read it that way, and, if it is done well, cannot otherwise properly appreciate the story.

This is a kind of storytelling, one we do not often find in southern fiction. Faulkner, for example, uses a great deal of his own personal experience in his fiction, but nobody reads, say, "The Bear" with the feeling that the author is asking us to watch him in the woods as a boy. It isn't told that way. Faulkner the writer usually keeps out of his fiction, in the sense of requiring us to keep in mind at all times a personal relationship between what is being described and the biographical author writing the description.

Wolfe, by contrast, wants us to do just that, and he tells his story so that we will do so. There is thus little or no "objectivity," and the deliberate and intense assertion of the writer's personality, with a view toward making us think and feel emotion about him and what he has done and thought, is very uncharacteristic of other southern authors. It is this, I think, that more than any other aspect of Wolfe's art accounts for the dislike that many good southern critics have felt toward him. Robert Penn Warren (who later became quite friendly with Wolfe) declared of *Of Time and the River* that it "illustrates once more the limitations, perhaps the necessary limitations, of an attempt to exploit directly and naively the personal experience and the self-defined personality in art." And he ended by pointing out that Shakespeare "merely wrote *Hamlet*; he was *not* Hamlet."

I rather doubt that the Warren who wrote the poetry he has been writing for the past two decades would have put the matter quite in that fashion if he were reviewing Wolfe's novel today. But the point is well taken, and I think it is an objective way of recording a reaction that was—perhaps not for Warren so much as for some of his contemporaries—not merely literary but personal. They didn't *like* Wolfe's personality; they were less than charmed by his continual assertions of uniqueness and sensibility, and thought him more than a little boorish and egotistical. The professional writer, they felt (and with considerable justification), didn't place himself on exhibition as a person, but let his art speak for him. Furthermore, that person on exhibition was hugely and passionately romantic and fascinated by the intensity of his own emotional responses. As Warren wrote, "The hero [of *Of Time and the River*] is really that nameless fury that drives Eugene. The book is an effort to name that fury, and perhaps by naming it, to tame it. But the fury goes unnamed and untamed." Warren and his contemporaries had no objection to the presence of fury in fiction. But they felt emphatically that the fury should take the form of fiction, not the author's feelings about himself and his personal experience.

I once attempted to account for the presence of this subjective, autobiographical assertion of personality in the Wolfe novels by noting the difference between Wolfe's background and early life and that of almost all his southern contemporaries. He came from a family that, as he portrays them, had little sympathy with intellectual interests and a tradition of literary sensibilities. The result was that he was led to turn his deepest feelings inward, to erect a barrier between the outside world and himself, and to develop a stern defensiveness about his literary and intellectual interests. With no public outlet for his feelings, the result was pent-up emotions and a fierce self-preoccupation that ultimately erupted in an intense fictional assertion of his own uniqueness and of the justification for it. If I may quote myself, "When the qualities of mind that made Thomas Wolfe into a novelist instead of a stone mason or a real-estate salesman did come fully into light, there was not surprisingly an explosive force to their emergence, a furious emotional subjectivity that could be disciplined only with great difficulty and always imperfectly."

I still believe there is considerable logic to that, so far as it goes, but upon reflection it seems too simple and too literal. The nature of artistic creativity, and the forms that it takes, are too complex and intricate to be ascribed to any such easy social formulation. I suspect that if there is an explanation of why Wolfe's artistic sensibilities sought the kind of expression they did, it would involve as much depth psychology as social studies, but the few attempts that have been made along that line have seemed less than impressive to me. Genius, Bernard DeVoto declared of Thomas Wolfe, is not enough, which may be true, but without it there would be no such interest as now exists in the novels and the man who wrote them, and because the genius was present, there are limits to logical explanation.

So perhaps it is best simply to accept, with considerable gratitude, that the man wrote as he did, and to note that there is little warrant for contending that the particular form that Wolfe's art took, with its passionate and direct assertion of personality, is somehow alien to his southern background. For while it is quite true that his southern literary contemporaries do not exhibit it, but on the contrary share with each other a marked formal objectivity, it is equally true that in other fields of activity there has been plenty of personal assertion on the southern scene. No one has ever suggested, for example, that Ellen Glasgow and James Branch Cabell were backward in writing quite personally and openly about themselves in their nonfictional writing, yet there is hardly much in the way of working-class experience in the background of those two Virginia patricians. Or consider more recent works such as James Agee's *Let Us Now Praise Famous Men*, or Willie Morris's *North Towards Home*, or such nineteenth-century productions as Mrs. Chesnut's *Diary*, first edited for publication by that lady herself, or the spate of memoirs of the Civil War period, some of them quite choleric, that were published during the late years of the last century and the early years of this. My point is not that they are comparable to Wolfe's writings, and still less that they are all equally works of art, but only that they are evidence that it has been by no means without precedent for a southerner to write directly and assertively about his own experience. Where Wolfe differs is that he did it in the form of autobiographical fiction—an important difference, but hardly a justification for considering him and his work as somehow not an outgrowth of southern experience.

I think it is wise, in considering the problem of Thomas Wolfe, and the South, to adopt Hugh Holman's insight: that Wolfe's subject is "the American self," that "this pattern of development is grounded in the South, but it is grounded in a South which is steadily expanding outward," that Wolfe's "fiction was determined by the Piedmont middle-class world which he knew," and that "when he moved from it, he moved outward to embrace the nation and to attempt to realize the promise of America." This is an old southern custom, you know: it began at least as early as Thomas Jefferson, and among its distinguished literary practitioners have been Mark Twain and the author of *Look Homeward, Angel*. So all in all, we would probably do well to take Thomas Wolfe as he comes; and the place he came from is Asheville, North Carolina.

The Fathers
and the Historical Imagination

C. HUGH HOLMAN

Allen Tate has written much about what he calls "the symbolic imagination" and the "angelic imagination," but it seems to me that one of the informing shapers of his unique novel *The Fathers* is what may be called the "historical imagination."[1]

The Fathers has always had a relatively small but very respectful audience; yet, although it has many of the qualities of a "coterie book"—particularly among southern critics who tend to see it as an almost perfect illustration of the agrarian concept of life—it has frequently baffled its readers to some extent and puzzled them in various ways.[2] Indeed, its readers and critics have had difficulty in coming to agreement about the meaning of the novel, about who its protagonist or protagonists are, and even about what happens at several crucial points in the novel itself. These issues have been discussed by a number of people, most persuasively, it seems to me, by Lynette Carpenter, who sees the central mode of the novel as being ambiguity about the nature and meaning of experience.[3] Many readers agree with Arthur

1. Allen Tate, "The Angelic Imagination," "The Symbolic Imagination," and "Our Cousin, Mr. Poe," in *Essays of Four Decades* (Chicago: Swallow Press, 1968), 385–446. These essays were first collected in Tate's *The Forlorn Demon* (Chicago: Regnery, 1953), wherein their theme was the defining principle of the volume. Part III of *Essays of Four Decades* similarly has this theme as its organizing focus. All references to Tate's essays will be to *Essays of Four Decades*, hereinafter called *Essays*.

2. See, for example, Thomas Daniel Young, Introduction, Allen Tate, *The Fathers and Other Fiction* (Baton Rouge: Louisiana State University Press, 1977), which emphasizes the fact that "*The Fathers* was completed while Allen Tate was deeply involved in the Agrarian movement" (p. ix).

3. Lynette Carpenter, "The Battle Within: The Beleaguered Consciousness

Mizener that "it is in fact a novel *Gone With the Wind* ought to have been," while others have seen it as a better example of Stark Young's *So Red the Rose*.[4] It has been viewed as the ultimate modernist novel, particularly by critics like Cleanth Brooks, who sees it as a condemnation of millennialism and the gnostic tendency of the modern world.[5] Radcliffe Squires has seen the novel as being "a triumph of the Jamesian viewpoint," but has also seen in it the marked influence of Ford Madox Ford.[6] I have looked at *The Fathers* as an example of a peculiarly American kind of *Bildungsroman*, one in which a minor-character spectator-narrator comes to an understanding of the cosmos and his role in it through what he witnesses happen to others rather than through what actually happens to him.[7] Walter Sullivan sees it as a condemnation of the inadequacies of the Protestant religion for an ordered and traditional society in the Old South.[8] Denis Donoghue sees the book as informed most meaningfully by Tate's distinction between the symbolic and the angelic imagination, represented in the novel by the Buchans and the Poseys.[9]

Some readers have seen Major Buchan as the protagonist of the novel; others have insisted that George Posey is its protagonist; in revising the ending in 1975, Tate said, "This revision gives the novel two heroes: Major Buchan, the classical hero, whose *hubris* destroys him; George Posey, who may have seemed

---

in Allen Tate's *The Fathers*," *Southern Literary Journal*, VIII (Spring, 1976), 3–23.

4. Arthur Mizener, Introduction, Allen Tate, *The Fathers* (Denver: Alan Swallow, 1960), ix; C. Hugh Holman, *The Immoderate Past: The Southern Writer and History* (Athens: University of Georgia Press, 1977), 56–62.

5. Cleanth Brooks, "Allen Tate and the Nature of Modernism," *Southern Review*, XII (October, 1976), 685–98.

6. Radcliffe Squires, *Allen Tate: A Literary Biography* (New York: Pegasus, 1971), 145.

7. C. Hugh Holman, "*Bildungsroman*, American Style," in *Windows on the World: Essays on American Social Fiction* (Knoxville: University of Tennessee Press, 1979), 168–97.

8. Walter Sullivan, "*The Fathers* and the Failures of Tradition," *Southern Review*, XII (October, 1976), 758–66.

9. Denis Donoghue, "The American Style of Failure," in his *The Sovereign Ghost: Studies in Imagination* (Berkeley: University of California Press, 1976), 114–19.

to some readers the villain, is now clearly a modern romantic hero."[10] The question arises, however, of whether Allen Tate, in 1975, is an authoritative witness about the nature and meaning of a book he created in 1938. Certainly others, including Lynette Carpenter and me, have insisted that the real action of the story is taking place in the spectator-narrator Lacy Buchan, and they are not likely to be persuaded by Tate's long-after-the-fact statement. But the fact remains that *The Fathers* has elicited much and very various criticism ranging from Mizener's early brilliant exposition of the novel as an example of the public versus the private life to contemporary insistences, such as Sullivan's, that it dramatizes the modern existential dilemma.[11]

There is, however, an aspect of the novel that has largely been ignored and that, combined with many of the technical aspects that critics have pointed out, goes a substantial distance toward explaining its bewildering structure and explicating its intended meaning. This aspect is that Allen Tate in writing *The Fathers* was, consciously or unconsciously, using the conventions, the devices, and some of the methods of the standard historical novel. But he modified them not only by his poetic style but also by the use of a Jamesian or Fordian structure in such a way that he expressed the essential structural meaning of the historical novel in new, interesting, and very valuable ways. In short, I believe that *The Fathers* is an American *Bildungsroman* with a spectator-narrator who is the ultimate subject of the book and who experiences the events of history—in particular those of

10. Allen Tate, "Preface: Caveat Lector," *The Fathers and Other Fiction* (Rev. ed.; Baton Rouge: Louisiana State University Press, 1977), xxi. All citations of *The Fathers* will be to this edition. So far as I have been able to determine, the text of the revised edition is identical to that of the 1938 Putnam edition and the 1960 Swallow edition, except for a serious modification of the last paragraph of the 1938 edition and the addition of a new paragraph (p. 306 of Putnam and Swallow and pp. 306–307 of the LSU edition).

11. Mizener's essay "*The Fathers* and Realistic Fiction," *Accent*, VII (Winter, 1947), 101–109, was republished in the *Sewanee Review*, LXVII (Autumn, 1959), 604–13. In its expanded, and best, form it constitutes Chap. XIII of Mizener's *The Sense of Life in the Modern Novel* (Boston: Houghton Mifflin, 1964), 267–87, and is used in something fairly close to its original form as the introduction to the Swallow edition of *The Fathers*.

southern history—in such a way that those historical events become his instructors in finding a way of life. What the protagonist witnesses is, of course, a primarily domestic pattern of events, but he sees them through the frame of an historical view. This theory of the novel suggests that Tate has achieved, either consciously or unconsciously, a major and important displacement of the typical Scott hero—a displacement that accounts for much of the ambiguity, the meaning, and the poetic beauty of his novel.

In one sense, *The Fathers* is a reconstruction in fictional form of Tate's personal family history. His mother had been born in Fairfax County, Virginia, in a farmhouse built to replace Pleasant Hill, an estate that was burned during the Civil War. This estate had been owned by his ancestor Major Lewis Bogan, whom Tate represents as Major Buchan in the novel. Radcliffe Squires insists convincingly that George Posey is based upon Tate's brother Benjamin, who had a successful business career and became rich.[12] In a note on the novel published in 1975, Tate said, "I still do not know where the 'plot' of *The Fathers* came from. I once thought I had found it in the court records of Fairfax County, in a deed-of-trust from my great-grandfather to one of his sons for the benefit of his daughter, my grandmother: this deed proved by inference that my great-grandfather did not wholly trust his son-in-law."[13]

Another possible source for the idea of this novel may have come from Tate's association, during the time it was being formulated, with Ellen Glasgow and in particular his reading of her early novel *The Battle-Ground*. Tate met Glasgow at the Southern Writers Conference, which was held at Charlottesville, Virginia, on October 23 and 24, 1931. He liked her very much, called her "Miss Ellen" in deference to her commanding position, and was pleased with her presentation of the formal keynote address.[14] This meeting ripened into an acquaintance and

12. Squires, *Allen Tate*, 14, 22, 135, 145.
13. Tate, *The Fathers*, 14.
14. E. Stanly Godbold, Jr., *Ellen Glasgow and the Woman Within* (Baton Rouge: Louisiana State University Press, 1972), 185–87.

resulted in a substantial exchange of letters between Tate and Glasgow in the 1930s and in visits from the Tates to her home. Tate began to read her novels as they were published and to praise them highly. She was particularly delighted with his remarks about *The Sheltered Life*.[15] When Glasgow was unable to present a paper she had agreed to read to the Modern Language Association at its annual meeting in 1936, Tate read it for her.[16] In March, 1933, she sent Tate the first four books in the Old Dominion Edition of her novels, including *The Battle-Ground*, and she wrote Tate, "Of the first four, *Virginia* is my favorite, and *The Battle-Ground* was the most popular, especially in the South."[17] In April she wrote Tate in response to his remarks about her books, saying, "*The Battle-Ground*, one of my very earliest books, has always held its place in the South, with a still earlier book called *The Voice of the People*."[18] During this time Tate abandoned the biography of Robert E. Lee on which he had been working, explaining in a letter to John Peale Bishop that Lee was "profoundly cynical of all action for the public good," and he began work on a novel, *Ancestors of Exile*, in which he had attempted to contrast the fundamental differences between the aristocrats of the Tidewater and the pioneers of the frontier.[19] In June, 1933, Tate sent Ellen Glasgow the first chapter of *Ancestors of Exile*, and her response was in her own terms "immediate and complete and enthusiastic." She saw Tate as doing here something quite similar to what she tried to do in her own fiction, and she compared his attempt to establish a union of the Scotch-Irish and the Tidewater with what she was attempting to do in her work in progress, *Vein of Iron*.[20] Allen Tate and Ellen Glasgow knew each other, respected each other, and saw themselves as working in similar traditions. Tate's "Ode to the Confederate Dead" was a poem which Ellen Glasgow admired

15. *Ibid.*, 191; Blair Rouse (ed.), *Letters of Ellen Glasgow* (New York: Harcourt, Brace, 1958), 139–40.

16. Godbold, *Ellen Glasgow*, 228.

17. Rouse (ed.), *Letters of Ellen Glasgow*, 129, 130.

18. *Ibid.*, 134.

19. Tate, *The Fathers*, xi.

20. Rouse (ed.), *Letters of Ellen Glasgow*, 136–37.

enormously and of which she said, "That is, I think, a great poem, because it strips away not only appearances but experience itself, and bears some dark and nameless quality of being."[21] She was sympathetic with his view of the South and of southern history, and she saw marked similarities between her views and his.

The Battle-Ground deals with two Virginia families just before and during the Civil War. It is an account of the disruption of the established culture of the Old South through the coming of that war. It opens with a long section dealing with Christmas at Chericoke in which a richly detailed picture of the customs and ideals of the Old South is presented through a ceremonial occasion in precise and loving detail, an introduction not unlike the opening chapters of Cooper's *The Pioneers*. Both books center on traditional communal ceremonies through which their authors portray the quality of the life of the people at the time of the action of the story and reveal the special nature of a particular culture—in Cooper's case, the settler's world on the banks of Lake Otsego in the 1790s; in Ellen Glasgow's, the aristocratic Virginia culture in the 1850s. In a similar fashion Part I of *The Fathers*, laid on the day of the funeral of Lacy Buchan's mother and containing a long flashback to a southern tournament, serves the purpose of defining the quality and nature of the life of a world soon to be disrupted by war.

In Glasgow's novel, the Civil War through the eruption of new forces destroys or radically converts the nature of its culture. She said in a letter while she was writing the novel, "I want . . . to make . . . a picture of varied characters who lived and loved and suffered during those years, and to show the effects of the times upon the development of their natures."[22] In the second half of the novel, Glasgow follows Dan Montjoy, a volunteer in the Confederate Army, from the opening of the conflict to his return to a devastated home and the difficult task of reconstructing a new life for himself and the other survivors. Thus she carries the action of the Civil War much further than Tate does,

21. *Ibid.*, 229.
22. *Ibid.*, 30.

since the conclusion of *The Fathers* comes on July 21, 1861. However, the references to battles and military actions at the opening of the war are much the same in the two novels, and both writers assume that the reader knows the military history and the geography of Virginia well enough to be able to identify actions as much as they need to be identified to understand the stories. For example, in *The Fathers*, immediately after a reference to Manassas Junction and the capturing of the armory at Harper's Ferry, Lacy Buchan says, "But what actually came next, what seemed so important at the time of its happening, I cannot remember, though I might consult the books and bring back the true order of events."[23] In *The Battle-Ground* Glasgow represents the battle of First Manassas and the forced winter march to Romney as a young recruit's bewildered and confused initiation into the realities of war. In Tate's case, the confusion and uncertainty results from the narrative's being the memories of a sixty-five-year-old man thinking back to his fifteenth year and trying to reconstruct what is significant to him in the present about that past.

In *The Battle-Ground* Glasgow was attempting, as she said, to create "an evocation of a lost way of living."[24] "What interested me, however," she said, "was not so much the historical incidents (though I was careful to verify these in the smallest particular) as the deeper effects of that desperate, if fantastic, struggle upon the characters of a civilization."[25] In her long study of these characters and this civilization, she ultimately found, she said, that the culture of the Old South was "shallow-rooted at best, since, for all its charm and its good will, the way of living depended, not upon its own creative strength, but upon the enforced servitude of an alien race."[26] In *The Fathers* essentially this same subject matter is pursued intensely, and the shallow roots of the culture of the Old South are also revealed. In

23. Tate, *The Fathers*, 153.
24. Ellen Glasgow, *A Certain Measure* (New York: Harcourt, Brace, 1943), 6.
25. Ellen Glasgow, *The Battle-Ground*, Old Dominion Edition (New York: Doubleday, Doran, 1929), viii.
26. Glasgow, *A Certain Measure*, 13.

Tate's analysis, this weakness rests at least in part on the dark institution of slavery, but for him there exists also other and, he believes, more fundamental weaknesses in the old order that must fall, and he works very hard to portray these weaknesses.

Denis Donoghue has argued that the central subject of *The Fathers* is actually the contrast between two modes of the imagination, which Tate has defined in his critical essays, and that the novel, though ostensibly about the defeat of the Old South, is actually about "the defeat of the symbolic imagination by the angelic imagination. The symbolic imagination," Donoghue explains, "is terrestrial, familial, domestic, and historical; it maintains a special interest in the sustaining relation between man and place, a relation embodied in customs, rituals, forms, and civility. The angelic imagination is an act of will, it is alienated from the world and therefore whirls between two worlds, depending upon its own intensity to keep it going; scornful of existence, it makes a direct claim upon essence, and therefore aspires toward every version of ultimacy and the absolute."[27] If this interpretation of the novel as being ultimately about the act of creation is to be taken seriously—and I think that it must—then Tate is indeed doing a great deal more than making a comment, however sophisticated, on the social history of the Old South or even upon the effect of the Civil War. He is trying to make a larger and encompassing statement about the nature of experience, of imagination, and of knowledge; he is attempting to contrast two sharply different ways of looking at life. Accordingly, he is employing in *The Fathers* a collection of specific, physical, and concrete elements that taken together can serve as the symbols of an imaginative statement about the order of reality. Lacy Buchan is quite explicit about this aspect of the novel when he says, "In my feelings of that time there is a new element—my feelings now about that time: there is not an old man living who can recover the emotions of the past; he can only bring back the objects around which, secretly, the emotions have ordered themselves in memory, and that memory is not what

27. Donoghue, *The Sovereign Ghost,* 117–18.

happened in the year 1860 but is rather a few symbols, a voice, a tree, a gun shining on the wall—symbols that will preserve only so much of the old life as they may, in their own mysterious history, consent to bear."[28] It is in this respect, together with the specificity of metaphor and the concreteness of image which make up the surface of Lacy Buchan's recollections, that *The Fathers* most clearly reveals the poetic aspects of its author's imagination and writing.

The Scott form of the historical novel was almost perfectly suited both to what Ellen Glasgow was attempting in *The Battle-Ground* and to the much more sophisticated and intricate uses of that formula to which, I believe, Allen Tate put it, either consciously or unconsciously, in *The Fathers*. Scott chose with particular care the period in which he set each of his historical novels, selecting it for qualities directly associated with his concept of history. He sought an age of great contrast between two cultures, one dying but still strongly felt in the world, the other coming into being but not yet dominant. As he said of *Ivanhoe*, "The period . . . afford[ed] a striking contrast betwixt the Saxons, by whom the soil was cultivated, and the Normans, who still reigned in it as conquerors, reluctant to mix with the vanquished, or acknowledge themselves of the same stock."[29] It was Scott's basic method to locate his protagonist, always an imaginary personage, in the middle of this historical conflict, and, whenever possible, have him partake of both sides. This became a pattern with *Waverley*, wherein young Waverley is committed to the Lowland Scots, who represent the future, but strongly attracted emotionally to the Highlanders, who represent a passing world. In *Ivanhoe* Wilfred of Ivanhoe, the "disinherited knight," is a Saxon who has adopted the ways of the Norman conquerors and who has been on a Crusade with the Norman army. He is now disinherited and exists very literally between two worlds, accepted by neither, born of one, possessing the skills of the other. Scott explores with great thoroughness the impact of

28. Tate, *The Fathers*, 22.
29. Sir Walter Scott, *Ivanhoe*, Riverside edition of *Scott's Complete Works* (Boston: Houghton, Mifflin, 1923), I, xii.

events upon the life of such middle-of-the-road characters during moments of great tension in history. Inevitably such a protagonist becomes a passive figure.[30] For example, Nigel in *The Fortunes of Nigel* says that he is "a thing never acting, but perpetually acted upon . . . as passive and helpless as a boat that drifts without oar or rudder at the mercy of the winds and waves."[31] But however weak such a protagonist may be, his passivity is a function of Scott's view of history and of life. He sees historical man as the product of social forces, a person who stands in a time and place unique to his nationality and his manners, in most respects a product rather than a producer. Scott's interest in these shaping forces constitutes the special contribution that he made to the novel, but it is an interest not so much in the forces themselves as in the impact of those forces upon common men living under them.

Such a concept of the novel was peculiarly applicable to what Allen Tate wanted to do in *The Fathers*. It seems to me that he dramatized in the Buchans the nature, the order, the strengths, and the weaknesses of the Old South, and through them presented a way of looking at life and a special sort of facing of reality; and in the Poseys he represented the new world, the way of the future, the force that acts through history ultimately to triumph. Thus he reinterprets the most cataclysmic event in national history not so much as a conflict between North and South but as an event greatly accelerating the struggle of these two ways of life within the South itself. For it is important to remember that the Poseys are a southern family with southern family traditions, who have moved to a city and have lost the sense of community, family, and oneness together with the traditions and the customs that bind a family into a functioning unit. Hence Buchans and Poseys constitute symbolic statements that have an

30. Alexander Welsh, in *The Hero of the Waverley Novels* (New Haven: Yale University Press, 1963), makes a thorough examination of Scott's "passive" protagonists. Georg Lukács, in *The Historical Novel*, trans. H. and S. Mitchell (Boston: Beacon Press, 1963), also treats the "weak" hero—what an unfortunate translation calls the "mediocre" hero.

31. Sir Walter Scott, *The Fortunes of Nigel*, Riverside edition of *Scott's Complete Works* (Boston: Houghton, Mifflin, 1923), II, 79.

historical validity, an imaginative aesthetic validity, and a thematic validity when viewed as aspects of the public or private life, as well as a moral validity. They serve, as the symbolic imagination would have them serve, as concrete, specific, but inclusive embodiments not of any one of these things but of them all. They stand in one sense at the far end of a spectrum from allegory and yet do not lose their quality of suggesting interpretations at a variety of levels of meaning. In large part, this variety of levels of meaning is the result of Tate's act of converting the protagonist of the Scott novel, the middle-of-the-road hero of the traditional historical romance, from the role of actor, however helpless, in the current of events to the quite different role of being a spectator and a learner who does not himself significantly act.

In so doing, Tate created in *The Fathers* a novel that might almost be taken as a paradigm of a special American-style *Bildungsroman*. This form is one in which a spectator-narrator comes to an understanding of the nature of the world and develops a philosophy for living in it not by his own actions but by watching the actions of others. The spectator-narrator in such tales almost always tells them from a retrospective stance well after the events have occurred. He recounts what he saw and attempts to understand it and to find in it special meanings that he is free to describe. In the case of *Moby-Dick*, Ishmael tells us what he learned some years before from watching Ahab and the fatal cruise of the *Pequod*. In Hawthorne's *Blithedale Romance*, Coverdale, talking from a later time, describes the tragic events surrounding Zenobia at Blithedale. Jim Burden, in Willa Cather's *My Ántonia*, describes what he learned from watching the life of Ántonia Shimerda years before. F. Scott Fitzgerald's Nick Carraway, in *The Great Gatsby*, describes what he learned from watching the tragedy of Jay Gatsby.

In a similar way the narrator of *The Fathers*, Lacy Buchan, a boy of fifteen at the time of action of the novel, is at the time of its telling "an unmarried old man . . . [who] has a story to tell. Is it not something to tell, when a score of people whom I knew and loved, people beyond whose lives I could imagine no other

life, either out of violence in themselves or the times, or out of
some misery or shame, scattered into the new life of the modern
age where they cannot even find themselves?" In language that
almost constitutes a definition of this special American-style
Bildungsroman, Lacy says, "I mark the beginning of my maturity
with a scene, and another marks its completion, and you will
understand that neither of them properly speaking was an experience of my own, but rather something sheer, out of the
world, easier to bring back than the miseries and ecstacies of my
own life." He is equally clear about what he learned from what
he witnessed. He says, "There was of course no one moment
that it was all leading up to, and that piece of knowledge about
life, learned that day, has permitted me to survive the disasters
that overwhelmed other and better men, and to tell their story.
Not even death was an instant; it too became a part of the cease-
less flow, instructing me to beware of fixing any hope, or some
terrible lack of it, upon birth or death, upon love or the giving in
marriage."[32]

This process of interpreting actions and declaring their meaning is, of course, made possible by the double perspective of Lacy
Buchan. The story that Lacy tells is what he witnessed, stated as
a function of the meaning it had in the process of his maturing.
Lacy is very thoroughly caught in the conflicting forces of the
narrative. He is a Buchan, raised in the heart of a family that
rested on order and tradition, that lived what Mizener has called
the public life, rich in ritual, ceremony, and ceremonial behavior
and language. But it is a family that found its meaning almost
exclusively in the past, a family that did things because that was
how they had always been done, a family that was insensitive to
the winds of change and resistant to the modifications essential
to living in the future. Yet Lacy is from the beginning enamored
of his brother-in-law George Posey, who comes from a totally
different kind of family. Posey represents the personal and private
self as opposed to a collective and public self, the modern and
the new as opposed to the old way of life. In a visionary moment

32. Tate, *The Fathers*, 5, 117–18, 101.

Lacy sees that "the only expectancy that he [George Posey] shares with humanity is the pursuing grave, and the thought of extinction overwhelms him because he is entirely alone." George lives a modern existential existence trapped in the loneliness of his individual self. The outside world lacks meaning for him. He was, Lacy declared, "a force that did not recognize the rules of his game." And yet Posey has, as the new and the modern always has for the very young, a powerful emotional appeal for Lacy Buchan. Despite the long accumulation of terrible things that George does, Lacy has for him a love greater than that which he has for any other man. Tate, in the 1975 commentary on the novel, stated this relationship in these words: "George will permit Lacy to survive in a new world in which not all the old traditions, which Lacy partly represents, are dead."[33]

Lacy Buchan is the passive Scott hero in whom the meaning of the conflict of the old and the new is realized in his attempt to interpret the events he witnessed. The result of his witnessing these events and his attempts to describe them places him in a very complex and ambiguous position, for, like Wilfred of Ivanhoe, he partakes deeply and fundamentally both of the old and of the new, and he is in a true and almost painfully tragic sense the man in the middle, the man born between the Old South and the New, the person caught between the demands of the public world and the modern solipsistic self, the person caught between a sense of the symbolic imagination and the obsessive demands of the angelic imagination.

Thus Allen Tate has constructed a novel with a fundamental Scott-like conflict, a conflict between two opposing ways of life. Like Scott, he feels a strong affection for the dying old culture, but also like Scott, he sees that it must go, no matter how much he may dislike the new. This conflict of two cultures is dramatically accelerated by an historical event, the Civil War. But Tate substitutes for Scott's passive protagonist a spectator-narrator recounting a retrospective narrative and brooding on its meanings. By so doing he is able to take the concrete materials of his

33. *Ibid.*, 267–68, 44, 314.

narrative and invest them with a wealth and a wide range of symbolic values, values that include the historical but also clearly transcend it. In the modification that Tate made in the structure of the traditional historical novel, he found a uniquely powerful and aesthetically satisfying way of presenting the fundamental situation of the Scott historical romance and at the same time giving it multiple levels of meaning and a deep and haunting resonance.

Walker Percy
and the Myth of the
Innocent Eye

∾

PANTHEA REID BROUGHTON

In *The Moviegoer* Walker Percy's narrator Binx Bolling, while traveling on a bus from Chicago to New Orleans, observes a young man whom he can immediately describe as a romantic. He explains: "The poor fellow. He has just begun to suffer from it, this miserable trick the romantic plays upon himself: of setting just beyond his reach the very thing he prizes" (Mg, 215).[1] Binx's definition, of course, harkens back to Denis de Rougemont, who suggests that in the West an experience is romantic only when obstacles prevent fulfillment of desire, when the thing prized remains out of reach. But the interesting point about Percy and this concept of romanticism is that it also applies to his concept of who the novelist is; for Percy speaks as if the novelist too must put beyond his reach the world that he prizes. Thus, Percy describes the novelist as a "somewhat estranged and detached person whose business it is to see things and people as if he had never seen them before" (MB, 11).

Only by putting himself at a certain remove from the world, the theory goes, can the novelist see the world clearly enough to make it visible to his readers. With Percy, the outsider can see

1. References to Percy's five books will be included parenthetically in the text of this paper and abbreviated accordingly: Mg: *The Moviegoer* (New York: Farrar, Straus, and Giroux, 1967); LG: *The Last Gentleman* (New York: Farrar, Straus, and Giroux, 1966); LR: *Love in the Ruins* (New York: Farrar, Straus, and Giroux, 1971); MB: *The Message in the Bottle: How Queer Man Is, How Queer Language Is, and What One Has to Do with the Other* (New York: Farrar, Straus, and Giroux, 1975); L1: *Lancelot* (New York: Farrar, Straus, and Giroux, 1977).

94

better than the insider because visibility is contingent upon separation. The corollary assumption is that ordinary folk are so sunk in, or adjusted to, everyday experience that the world they inhabit is invisible to them; their surroundings, belongings, hands, wives, existences, cannot be *seen*. Given such assumptions, only a wayfarer or pilgrim or exile or castaway or amnesiac or even a Martian can really *see* things as they are. The danger to the amnesiac (like the romantic or the novelist) would be settling down or becoming involved or allowing his desires to be fulfilled.

By insisting that the novelist be detached and estranged—that is, one to whom fulfillment is denied—Percy echoes Binx Bolling's definition of a romantic. But Percy's concept of a novelist is romantic in a second and, for my purposes here, even more crucial sense that has to do with *seeing*; for Percy talks as if, regardless of craft or wisdom, simply *seeing* the world afresh conveys meaning and understanding to his art. In a recent "self-interview" entitled "Questions They Never Asked Me" Percy writes, "This may be the main function of art in this peculiar age; to reverse the devaluation [of commonplace things]."[2] Thus, because the artist can "see things and people as if he had never seen them before," he can convey wonder before reality and make us see the world as it is. And seeing, Percy implies, is sufficient unto itself.

Seeing is not, however, as simple as it may sound. The essay "The Loss of the Creature" (MB, 46–63) explains how symbolic packaging intervenes between human beings and reality so that we see "it" (*i.e.*, the symbol) rather than the thing itself. Apparently some sort of disruption (being asked to dissect a dogfish instead of to analyze a Shakespearean sonnet) or discovery (getting lost on the way to Mexico City and finding an "unspoiled" Indian village) or surprise (Crusoe seeing a footprint in the sand) is necessary before experience can be encountered face-to-face and seen afresh. Thus "The Loss of the Creature" illus-

2. Walker Percy, "Questions They Never Asked Me: A Self-Interview," *Esquire*, LXXXVIII (December, 1977), 172.

trates how difficult it is for modern man to circumvent symbolic packaging and reclaim the vision of a more innocent eye.

As Percy talks about *seeing* as an end, he shows himself to be very much a part of the romantic tradition that emerged in Europe and England during the nineteenth century. Despite its foreign roots, however, this tradition of equating sight with insight has been appropriated by the American mind, so that now it seems uniquely American. The most complete treatment of what might be called this Americanization of romanticism may be found in Tony Tanner's *The Reign of Wonder: Naivety and Reality in American Literature.* Tanner begins by explaining how central to nineteenth-century English romanticism was the notion of the supremacy of the naïve vision. Tanner insists that to Rousseau the naïve vision, with its childlike sense of wonder, was a preparation for developing adult capacities of judgment, interpretation, and analysis. The romantics, however, adapted from Rousseau the concept of the naïve vision without retaining his sense of its limitations; they spoke as if the child's vision was sufficient unto itself. Tanner explains:

> The distrust of judgement and analysis, the conviction of the need for a renewed sense of wonder and admiration, a new stress on 'the passive susceptibilities,' a longing to feel the wholeness of the universe rather than merely understand it—almost inevitably writers who embraced this cluster of ideas fastened on the child's relationship with nature as a symbol of their own aspirations. The child's wondering eye offered the romantic writer an avenue back to a reality from which he fast felt himself becoming alienated. By recapturing a naive vision he might once again enjoy an untrammelled intimacy with nature. There would be a new reverence, a new quietude, a new sense of total glory. Thus we find the myth of the 'innocent eye' recurring throughout the [nineteenth] century.[3]

Tanner sees that "the recurring references to the superior vision of the child testify to a tremendous hunger to discover a new

3. Tony Tanner, *The Reign of Wonder: Naivety and Reality in American Literature* (Cambridge, England: Cambridge University Press, 1965), 7.

access to reality, a new habit of wonder." The irony is that "Rousseau would not have understood at all."[4]

Though interest in the innocent eye did recur throughout the nineteenth century in Europe and England, there it was one idea among many. In America, however, it took hold as the preferred and nearly exclusive way of apprehending reality. Tanner writes that "from the start 'wonder' was put to much more far-ranging uses in American writing than in any other literature." His thesis is that "the stance of wonder has *remained* a preferred way of dealing with experience and confronting existence among American writers."[5] Tanner discusses American writers from Emerson to Hemingway, and as a final illustration of his point he quotes from Bellow's *Dangling Man* and Percy's *The Moviegoer*.[6] These two contemporary novels, Tanner maintains, could "only be American," because only in America has wonder remained a meaningful approach to reality.[7]

Tanner sees in Percy simply a continuation of that deep-seated, uniquely American tradition of wonder and naïveté; but I do not feel that Percy's concern for the naïve vision is as naïve as Tanner would have us believe. Certainly it is true that Percy's own statements about the function of art and the need for circumventing symbolic packaging do testify to just such a sense of the supremacy of the innocent eye. But there is a real danger in taking, as I believe Tanner does, what Percy's characters say at face value. And there is a further danger in taking what Percy says as a final explanation for what he does, for Percy the theorist and Percy the fictionist wear very different masks.

The question of why there is such a radical split between what Percy says and what he does is beyond the scope of this essay, but I would like to suggest that its sources may be found in the curious dialectic of Percy's life. For Percy has found himself first

4. *Ibid.*, 8–9.
5. *Ibid.*, 10.
6. Tanner quotes from that passage [Mg, 42] in which Binx says that he will not be "distracted from the wonder."
7. Tanner, *The Reign of Wonder*, 11.

one thing and then another, at one pole and then another, without any way to live in a middle ground. He was first his parents' son, and then after their early and violent deaths, his Uncle Will's protégé.[8] He was first a medical doctor, then a novelist, first a scientist, then a humanist. It seems to me no wonder then that as philosopher and novelist Percy would continue that radical division which has typified his life.

I must qualify that hypothesis, however, by noting that Walker Percy himself acknowledges no such division between his saying and doing. Instead, Percy speaks of a development from the limited knowledge of science to the fuller knowledge of art. In an interview he explained:

> I see my own writing as not really a great departure from my original career, science and medicine, because . . . science will bring you to a certain point and then no further, it can say nothing about what a man is or what he must do. And then the question is, how do you deal with man? And if you are an anthropologist in the larger sense, interested in man, how do you study him? And it seemed to me that the novel itself was a perfectly valid way to deal with man's behavior.[9]

In other words, the scientist or theorist is limited to partial knowledge, but the artist or novelist can deal with the whole human being. Later in that same interview Percy refers to Kierkegaard to make a further distinction:

> [Kierkegaard] wrote a wonderful, a very important essay called "The Difference Between a Genius and an Apostle." It's very, very important. He said a genius could see the world *sub specie eternitatis*, the way things are in general, and he can tell people this—the way things are in general—but he did not have the authority to come to anybody and tell them any news. . . . Where-

---

8. Walker Percy and his two brothers were left in the care of their guardian William Alexander Percy, whom they called "Uncle Will," though he was their father's first cousin, and not his brother.

9. John Carr (ed.), "Rotation and Repetition: Walker Percy Interviewed by John Carr," in *Kite-Flying and Other Irrational Acts: Conversations with Twelve Southern Writers* (Baton Rouge: Louisiana State University Press, 1972), 40.

as an apostle is precisely a man who has the authority to come
and tell somebody the news. . . . A novelist least of all has the
authority to edify anyone or tell them good news, to pronounce
Christ King.[10]

I have quoted these passages at some length in order to suggest
that Percy sees, not the split I have referred to, but rather a continuum. In fact he sees a hierarchy of kinds of knowledge extend-
ing from the limited to the absolute. Lowest in the hierarchy is
the scientist or theorist who can make only a limited observation. Higher is the novelist or genius who can show experientially
"how things are." But highest of all is the prophet or apostle
who can convey news of another transcendent realm.

Perhaps then Percy would say of his own statements about the
revelatory power of the innocent eye that, like any scientific or
theoretical observation, they represent only partial understandings. More complete understandings of human existence can be
found in art, but only faith can discover ultimate truth. Thus
Percy would see it as perfectly consistent that his own art reveals
the limitations of his various theories. Therefore his art, while it
never attempts to offer news or Truth, does supersede the more
limited knowledge offered by his theories.

Percy's novels, for instance, show us a great deal about detachment and vision. As we have seen, Percy's theories suggest that
the artist can see better if he is somewhat detached and that the
ordinary person can see better when some disruption forces him
to "come to" or return to his authentic self. Percy acknowledges
that "in what sense he has come to himself, how it transforms
his relationship with his family, his business, his church, is of
course the burden of the novel" (MB, 109). And Percy's novels
do deal with the aftermath of such experiences. Yet repeatedly
they show that coming to oneself and seeing afresh does not redeem; in fact, it has no more lasting an effect than Binx's car
accident which promises to dispell the malaise. "Farewell forever,
malaise," Binx proclaims (Mg, 127) as he discovers his love for

10. *Ibid.*, 46–47.

Sharon is now "invincible" (Mg, 125). But as soon as Sharon is won, Binx discovers "I do not love her so wildly as I loved her last night" (Mg, 135), and the malaise threatens to settle in again.

Furthermore, Percy the novelist allows each of his protagonists to test Percy the theorist's assumption that the alienated perspective is the accurate one; thus each distances himself from the everyday and the familiar. Binx Bolling has exiled himself in Gentilly; Will Barrett has gone north; Thomas More puts a lapsometer between himself and his patients; and Lancelot Lamar sees only the slice of life visible through a cell window; "Have you noticed [he asks] that the narrower the view the more you can see?" (L1, 3). Each of these characters wishes to *see* better, but the novels show what Percy's nonfiction does not acknowledge: that seeing well does not redeem and that being outside the world means being incomplete. For the problem is that in trying to gain perspective, each protagonist so abstracts, as More phrases it, "himself from himself and from the world around him, seeing things as theories and himself as a shadow, that he cannot, so to speak, reenter the lovely ordinary world" (LR, 34).

Probably the best metaphor for that situation occurs in *The Last Gentleman* when Will Barrett buys a telescope in order to get the ordinary world back into perspective. Barrett expects the telescope to penetrate to the heart of things and reclaim for him lost sovereignty over his own existence. In other words, he is acting out (albeit with modern technology) the romantic assumption that in *seeing* is salvation. Attributing magical properties to the telescope, he sets up the precision instrument on a window sill of the New York City YMCA and focuses it upon a disc of bricks across Central Park: "He slapped his leg. It was as he had hoped. Not only were the bricks seen as if they were ten feet away; they were better than that. It was better than having the bricks there before him. They gained in value. Every grain and crack and excrescence became available. Beyond any doubt, he said to himself, this proves that bricks, as well as other things, are not as accessible as they used to be. Special measures were needed to recover them. The telescope recovered them" (LG, 31).

Here we see that the telescope is a superb stratagem for *seeing*.

It delivers the bricks in astonishingly precise detail. But, the fact remains, it delivers only bricks; yet Will Barrett expects (as Percy the theorist seems to) that *seeing* will recover not just the material under observation but being itself. Barrett's intentions are so obvious that his normally obtuse analyst sees what he is up to; he asks Barrett if he wants to become a "see-er. 'After all [Dr. Gamow explains] a seer is a see-er, one who can see. Could it be that you believe that there is some ultimate hidden truth and that you have the magical means for obtaining it?' " (LG, 37). Barrett laughs and shrugs his shoulders, but apparently that is precisely what he does believe. The telescope does recover things and enable Barrett to see afresh, but the book suggests that such vision is, after all, rather a trivial end. As Dr. Gamow's rhetoric makes clear, it is absurd to equate being a see-er with being a seer.

The Last Gentleman further shows that an absolutely fresh, utterly clear vision of things bears no necessary relation to the quality of existence. In fact, because seeing requires a distanced perspective, vision tends to remove a person from *being*. Rather than enabling one to reenter the lovely ordinary world, clear vision intensifies the condition Binx Bolling terms "the malaise," or "the pain of loss [in which the] world is lost to you, the world and the people in it, and there remains only you and the world and you are no more able to be in the world than Banquo's ghost" (Mg, 120). Barrett's purchase of the telescope illustrates the point, for, though he was convinced "that his very life would be changed if he owned the telescope" (LG, 29) and though he does discover not just bricks but a beautiful young girl through the telescope's sights, he must leave the instrument behind before he can meet the girl. Barrett's use of the telescope to recover bricks and "things" serves as an analogue for the sort of "special measures" Percy's protagonists use to see and understand the world. But such stratagems for *seeing* only heighten the malaise and render the characters in some way even less in the world than Banquo's ghost. Thus having traveled out to find and see the lovely ordinary world, these characters desperately try to return and live in it.

Throughout Percy's fiction characters attempt various strata-

gems designed to gain them "access to being" (MB, 51).[11] The
minor characters purchase things, adapt roles, and follow for-
mulas in pathetic attempts to bring some meaning to their lives.
When Percy's major characters encounter others who place faith
in such inauthentic measures, their necks prickle or their scalps
bristle as signals that they *see* the artificiality and futility of such
devices. But the major characters who can *see* so clearly need
also to be able to *be* in this world. They search for stratagems
that will allow them to overcome distance and return to the
world.

One such means for reentry is crisis. Tom More suggests: "At
that time [the old auto age] the only treatment of angelism, that
is excessive abstraction of the self from itself, was recovery of
the self through ordeal" (LR, 37). Another means that works in
roughly comparable ways to make people "real," in Kate Cutrer's
terms, is sex. Sutter Vaught has an elaborate theory that fornica-
tion is the "sole channel to the real" (LG, 372). To him it is the
"sole portal of reentry" (LG, 345) for abstracted human beings.
Both ordeal and sex serve to immerse one totally in the present;
thus they overcome abstraction, but only temporarily; for neither, by definition, can be sustained.

Lancelot Lamar remarks, "There is no joy on this earth like
falling in love with a woman and managing at the same time the
trick of keeping just enough perspective to see her fall in love
too" (L1, 122). But throughout Percy's fiction, we see that that is
an impossible trick, for the distance necessary for keeping one's
perspective precludes *being* and therefore being able to fall in
love. Even Sutter Vaught has to acknowledge "The Failure of
Coitus as a Mode of Reentry into the Sphere of Immanence from
the Sphere of Transcendence" (LG, 65). In other words, the fic-

11. For further discussion of the concept of "stratagems" see my introduction to my edited collection entitled *Stratagems for Being: Essays on the
Writings of Walker Percy* (Baton Rouge: Louisiana State University Press,
1979). For a basic acquaintance with Percy's writings, the reader is referred,
to that volume and to Martin Luschei's *The Sovereign Wayfarer: Walker
Percy's Diagnosis of the Malaise* (Baton Rouge: Louisiana State University
Press, 1972).

tion shows that *being* and *seeing* (in the terms these characters strive for) tend to cancel each other out.

Nevertheless, not only Lancelot but all Percy's protagonists think that they can manage the trick of at once *being* in the world and keeping their perspective. They suspect that such a combination of *being* and *seeing* is best achieved through the experiences Kierkegaard defined as "repetition" and "rotation." In the words of a minor character in *Love in the Ruins*, such experiences "add piquancy to the observer factor" (LR, 164); in other words, they promise to conjoin *being* with *seeing*. But both rotation and repetition depend upon surprise—rotation on the unexpectedly fresh experience, repetition upon the unexpectedly familiar experience—and thus also are impossible to sustain. As Binx Bolling realizes, "Places get used up by rotary and repetitive use" (Mg, 145).

Nevertheless, each of Percy's major characters still searches for the ideal human condition that would somehow allow him to be far enough from the world to see it and yet simultaneously be enough in the world to experience it. He seems to expect that condition in particular moments triggered by catastrophe. Again and again Percy depicts such moments: the experiences of the commuter after the wreck of the eight-fifteen, the soldier after the bullet left him barely alive, or the husband after discovering his wife's infidelity. Apparently, the intent is to examine the actual character of such vision-clearing experiences. Thus Percy's fiction tests the assumption that with knowledge (*i.e.*, familiarity) there can be no news (*i.e.*, revelation) and that therefore some disruptive experience is necessary in order that sight break through into insight. Such a disruption is a piquant stratagem added to the observer factor that recycles knowledge as news. The assumption is that only through such a disruption can one experience a work of art or understand a Shakespearean sonnet or actually *see* the Grand Canyon.

Percy explicitly claims such ideas as his own in "The Loss of the Creature." The museum scene in *The Last Gentleman* is apparently intended to illustrate them. Will Barrett finds happy people "worse off in their happiness in museums than anywhere else" (LG, 26). Because a museum packages art, it detaches the viewer and seems to accomplish the loss of the creature or loss of the experience of the art itself. Barrett has discovered that in a museum "it is impossible to look at a painting simply so: Man-looking-at-a-painting, *voilà!*—no, it is necessary to play a trick such as watching a man who is watching, standing on his shoulders, so to speak" (LG, 26–27).

But such tricks are not always effective in circumventing the museum's packaging. Often some other sort of piquancy must be added before the paintings become truly visible and alive. In the Metropolitan Museum of Art Barrett notices that public "secretion" from all the culturally advantaged, self-conscious viewers actually prevents a perfectly lighted, properly hung Velázquez from being seen. But suddenly there is an accident in the museum: a workman falls and cannot for a time catch his breath. After what seems an interminable interval, however, he pulls himself up on Will Barrett's arm and begins to breathe. Percy describes the results: "It was at this moment that the engineer [Barrett] happened to look under his arm and catch sight of the Velázquez. It was glowing like a jewel! the painter might have just stepped out of his studio and the engineer, passing in the street, had stopped to look through the open door. The paintings could be seen" (LG, 28). Presumably, it took a near-catastrophe to clear the museumgoers' vision so that they could see the very art they had come to admire.

How are we to take this scene? Are we to conclude that the accident not only clears the air so that the painting can be seen but that *seeing* somehow makes the viewers more alive? Similarly, are we to assume that the telescope does deliver the world? Are we to envy Barrett because, as an amnesiac, "like the sole survivor of a bombed building, he had no secondhand opinions and he could see things afresh"? (LG, 11). Are we to think that rotations and repetitions make Binx Bolling's life meaningful? Are we to approve the sort of piquant stratagems Thomas More employs to intensify his life? Are we to envy Lancelot Lamar the vision-clearing experience he has when he discovers his wife's infidelity?

Clearly, to all the above, the answer is no. I think, in fact, that the quest for a vision-clearing experience is just as futile as what Percy calls the "dynamic quest for resplendent forms" (MB, 284) or the search for the proper credentials "certifying, so to speak, one's right to exist" (Mg, 7) or the search for a proper methodology in books like *How to Harness Your Secret Powers* (Mg, 24) or *Technique in Marriage* (Mg, 189), which promise to bring meaning to one's life. All of such stratagems are inefficacious because they attempt to find spiritual meaning through material means. Similarly, piquancy and sex only open one to participation in this world. They cannot serve as permanent answers to the problem of alienation. Rotation and repetition do make vision and participation possible, but such momentary experiences of intense *being* and *seeing* are short-lived and, because they necessarily orient us to this world, cannot possibly help us to overcome spiritual alienation any more than a vision-clearing experience that restores the innocent eye can.

Of course, Percy's protagonists, like typical American romantics, want to believe that the innocent eye will reclaim the lost world and somehow accomplish their spiritual salvation. And sometimes vision promises to work that way. After all, it was when he came to himself while lying wounded in a ditch in Korea that the search first occurred to Binx Bolling. He explains, "I was onto something. I vowed that if I ever got out of this fix, I would pursue the search. Naturally, as soon as I recovered and got home, I forgot all about it" (Mg, 11). Throughout *The Moviegoer* Bolling cultivates and savors various eye-opening experiences, apparently believing that through them he can renew the search. Bolling explains that "the search is what anyone would undertake if he were not sunk in the everydayness of his own life. This morning, for example, I felt as if I had come to myself on a strange island. And what does such a castaway do? Why, he pokes around the neighborhood and he doesn't miss a trick" (Mg, 13). Bolling's problem throughout most of *The Moviegoer*, however, is that he only pokes around "the neighborhood." But being a castaway means understanding humankind's true predicament as alienation from our spiritual home. These ideas are developed in Percy's essay "The Message in the Bottle," wherein he defines a castaway so: "To be a castaway is to search for news from across the seas" (MB, 144). Clearly, the vision-clearing experience can open one to this world, but, unless it proceeds to a search for news from beyond this world, it grounds one inextricably to what Kierkegaard terms the "esthetic sphere." Presumably, with Bolling, only in the book's epilogue, after his marriage to Kate, is he truly able to renew the search and to live in what Kierkegaard calls the "religious" mode of existence.

While "wonder" involves opening oneself only to finite things and living in the esthetic sphere, a relationship such as Bolling establishes with Kate involves opening oneself to another spiritual being. Further, while wonder is passive, such an intersubjective relationship is active; while wonder is disengaged, intersubjectivity is involved and committed; wonder is naïve and nonintellectual while intersubjectivity engages the full human capacities for enjoyment, responsiveness, responsibility, wisdom, and love.

Each of Percy's first three novels ends with the establishment of such a relationship. Each protagonist discovers that true communion with another does enable him to transcend the particulars of his own finite existence. Through them we see something of the standard that remains implicit throughout Percy's fiction.[12]

That standard may be inferred from a comparison of the pro-

12. This essay was written before the publication of Percy's fifth novel, *The Second Coming* (New York: Farrar, Straus, and Giroux, 1980). This the latest novel returns not only to the characters of *The Last Gentleman* but to the stratagems of the first three novels. That is, the middle-aged Will Barrett of *The Second Coming* tests out, virtually on every page, the ways to escape everydayness I have outlined here. He tries ordeal, sex, rotation, and repetition, but none brings him into *being*. As an amnesiac, Allison sees the world with a wondrously innocent eye, but her existence is a limited, broken affair without Will. But the end of the book shows that only intersubjectivity or love can allow Will and Allison too to conjoin *being* with *seeing*. Thus *The Second Coming* reenacts quite explicitly the pattern I outline here for the first three novels.

tagonists at the novels' beginnings and at their ends. Such a comparison, I think, establishes that the wondrous innocent eye hardly offers the redemption of humankind. Certainly, Bolling's early refusal to be distracted from the wonder seems juvenile when compared to his later commitment to other people; near the end of *The Moviegoer* he explains to Kate: "There is only one thing I can do: listen to people, see how they stick themselves into the world, hand them along on ways in their dark journey and be handed along, and for good and selfish reasons" (Mg, 233). And similarly, Will's ability to *see* in the museum is trivial beside his ineffable experience in the hospital when, though he "did not know how he knew" (LG, 406), he nevertheless knows what the dying Jamie is saying. Clearly the early Sutter Vaught who could "only love a stranger" (LG, 183) is limited beside the Sutter who finally will wait for Will. And certainly, the early Thomas More, who needed the threat of catastrophe or the possibility of suicide in order to live, is pathetic; for he could capture life only through the imminence of death: "Seeing the blood [his own] I came to myself, saw myself as itself and the world for what it is, and began to love life" (LR, 97). That early More exhibits none of the psychic and spiritual strength of the More who five years later can live and love without "any such humbug as marked the past peculiar years of Christendom" (LR, 403).

Lancelot, of course, is another matter. Certainly, Lancelot's discoveries of his father's corruption and his wife's infidelity were eye-opening experiences. These discoveries cleansed away the fog and allowed Lance to *see*. But *seeing* did not cure Lance; in fact, it only confirmed his own sickness and culminated finally in the absolute detachment and clear focus with which he killed four people. Lance was so depraved that for him there was "no discovery, no flickering of interest, nothing at all, not even any evil" (Lı, 253) at the heart of evil.

Here I think Percy shows us what the vision-clearing experience will be unless it is contained within the context of love and faith. For Lance does *see*. He *sees* the folly and dishonesty and brutality of this world. He *sees* immorality so clearly in fact that he combats it with another immorality; to him there is nothing else. That is why his vision of a new order founded upon brute power is so depraved and hopeless.

At the end of *Lancelot* Percival knows there is another way. Lance is correct to say to him, "It will be your way or it will be my way" (L1, 257). That is, either *seeing* reveals the meaningless venality of this world and converts one to it or it convinces one of the limits of all that is finite. If the former, to quote Flannery O'Connor's misfit, there's "no pleasure but meanness." If the latter, there is pleasure in responding to the spirit in other human beings, in handing them along, and in searching for meaning beyond this world. In such pursuits, the fiction implies, can be our only meaning.

The contrived romantic stratagem of putting just beyond one's reach whatever one prizes is finally like the naïve romantic stratagem of wonder. For, in each, interest is contingent upon distance. And each, Percy's fiction shows, is predicated upon the assumption that meaning exists where it does not. Thus Percy's fiction hardly endorses his characters' frantic quest for a vision-clearing experience; rather it reveals its inadequacy. Whatever Percy says about the value of *seeing*, his fiction shows that seeing alone is meaningless. If Tanner is right about a continuing American tendency to value the innocent eye, I think that with Percy that tendency comes of age. For Percy does not continue it, he satirizes it and thus takes his place in a long line of Christian satirists whose art judges the world and its devices and finds them wanting.

The Clay Foot of
the Climber: Richard M. Nixon
in Perspective

JOHN SEELYE

I.

History is mostly, as the feminists lament, "his story," being in the words of Thomas Carlyle "the biography of great men." It is also an anatomy of error, a great book of mistakes from which today's great men may learn the lesson of the past. History is therefore the story of great men's failings and failures, which is to say that as literature it approximates tragedy. With Coleridge, Hegel, and G. B. Shaw we may doubt whether great men really do learn much from history, for they seem to be bound to repeat past errors, becoming thereby tragic rather than triumphant heroes; but with Samuel Butler we may be sure that when the great man turns historian it will be to rectify his mistakes by a process of revision, reforming his errors by justifying them. We have recently witnessed a powerful illustration of this truth in the fall of Richard M. Nixon, for whom history was a Guinness book of records to which he contributed a considerable list of presidential firsts. That is, Nixon saw the past as a pile of facts from the top of which the great man thrust his head and shoulders into the statistical future. He was, as he saw it, a Carlylean hero whose time had come, and in time it did, but not in the manner that he meant; nor were his concluding presidential firsts much to his liking either. And he may be expected to spend the rest of his life revising the facts of his political life, revisionist autobiography being very much in the American vein, which may be traced back to Ben Franklin.

Like so many of his inventions, Ben's book was but a new,

improved version of spiritual autobiography, a favorite Puritan genre, and it took its cast from another Puritan literary mode, providential (*i.e.*, revisionist) history. Neither form, it is important to note, accommodates a tragic view of life, with the single exception of William Bradford's *Of Plymouth Plantation*, which, if it does not actually frame the history of Plymouth as a tragedy, does in effect present it as such. But the great tradition, from Edward Johnson's *Wonder Working Providence* to Cotton Mather's *Magnalia Christi Americana*, is one of compiling evidence that the saints of Massachusetts are God's chosen people, proving on the national level what spiritual autobiography proves on the personal level, that the people are in a spiritual state of grace—howevermuch troubled and tormented the flesh. Such a people cannot come to tragic ends, for such flaws as they have are but enhancements of the larger whole. Puritan doctrine no longer has any particular relevance to American life, but much as "Redeemer Nation" became first the idea of Manifest Destiny and then the Marshall Plan, so we may observe the transformation of the idea of personal election from *electio dei* to *electio populi*, from whence Nixon drew his deep conviction of being holier-than-thou and his incredible powers of self-righteousness.

There remains, however, a missing link in the metamorphic progression from Franklin to Nixon, and that is Ragged Dick, Horatio Alger's contribution, who takes his name from Poor Richard, Franklin's persona grata who gave the world *The Way to Wealth*. What is popularly called the Horatio Alger story is a ritualized fiction based on the Franklin formula, a fabulization of the American Dream of success. As *Franklinad*, the Alger story is a further secularization of spiritual biography, Foxe's martyrs becoming foxy magnates, fictional *exempla* inspiring American youth to go and do likewise. As we shall see, Alger's was a formula with a difference, and although Richard M. Nixon is not a perfect Alger hero by any means, the Whittier-to-the-White-House saga is most certainly another American variation on the Dick Whittington theme. Moreover, the Alger connection is dramatically demonstrated by Nixon's greatest creation—Spiro

Agnew. Like Alger, Agnew was a nonentity who became a household word associated with acts of aggressive alliteration, but he
chiefly illustrates the *other* side of the American myth of success,
wherein *myth* connotes, not the truths that men live by, but the
fictions that leak at the seams. In Spiro Agnew's rise and fall we
have a high-speed paradigm of Nixon's own *agon*, illustrating
not only the fiction of the self-made man but the terrible truth
of the clay foot of the climber. Agnew's total performance demonstrates that opportunism is to opportunity in America what
permissiveness is to freedom, the man on the make also being on
the take.

There is an old story about the midwestern millionaire who
started out as a poor boy selling papers in the streets of Saint
Louis. He worked day and night until he had saved enough
money to build a little newsstand on a corner, and then he
worked even harder until he owned another little newsstand
and then another. In time, he bought a horse and wagon and
began delivering papers to his chain of newsstands, and by the
time he came of age he had saved enough money to take a vacation. So he booked passage on a steamboat down to New Orleans, where he met and married the madam of a whorehouse,
and that is how he became a millionaire. This is not necessarily
a true story, but there is a certain truth in it, dark with the cyni-
cism that the events of the past few years have imbued with an
unholy light. Like so many dirty jokes, it is an impudent refuta-
tion of accepted proprieties, like da-glo graffiti a luminescent
wall writing in dark places. You have to sell yourself to amount
to anything in America, and to do so amounts—whatever the
arrangement—to prostitution.

Hawthorne's "My Kinsman, Major Molineux," provides us
with a definitive fable in this latter regard, for on his frustrated
search through Boston for the rich relative who will give him a
hand up in life, young Robin encounters only one friendly person—a prostitute. Assuring him that "Major Molineux dwells
here," she tries to lure Robin into her house, and though the
moral to Hawthorne's dark tale seems to be that in America
young men cannot depend on help from above, there is a great

deal of validity in the prostitute's lie. Hawthorne's story ante-
dates the Alger story by a considerable period, having been first
published two years before Alger was born, but in terms of our
literature it provides an effective antidote to the rags-to-riches
formula. In the post-Alger period a number of American writers
came to precise and antagonistic terms with the Alger story.
From Mark Twain's *Adventures of Tom Sawyer* (and ragged
Huck) to Dreiser's *American Tragedy*, from Fitzgerald's *Great
Gatsby* to Nathanael West's *Cool Million*, and on to Schulberg's
What Makes Sammy Run?, "making it" in modern American
literature is an overreaching comedy darkening into tragedy, the
inevitable death of the perennial salesman of self.

It is important to recognize, however, that the anti-Alger strain
in American literature appears more frequently in our fiction,
and if the fact that Spiro Agnew has chosen to give his version of
the truth by means of a novel with a tragic denouement asserts
his Greek origins, it also testifies to his assimilation into our culture. Alger himself wrote mostly fiction, his lives of Garfield and
Lincoln for children quickly exhausting the catalog of those men
who actually did rise from poverty to presidential power. He was
thereby able to facilitate the presentation of what is essentially a
comic view of life, for though he placed his young heroes in realistic enough settings—whether the grinding poverty of rural life
or the desperate streets of the city—he endowed his fables with
a magical atmosphere, a Dickensian mood of marvel and miracle.
The typical Alger hero is a lad of humble circumstances but of
stalwart and sterling character, who performs some heroic deed
that brings him to the attention of a wealthy gentleman, a patron
who gives him that which is the desire of all Alger heroes, college
graduates, and ex-convicts—a new suit of clothes and a job. The
Alger hero, that is to say, inevitably and invariably gets what is
called "a break," and once again we may think of Spiro Agnew
being elevated by a similar stroke of good fortune, lifted from
the ranks of the PTA to the status of a VIP, enjoying the company of kings and comedians. But we should also remember
Hawthorne's nightmare antithesis, Robin's frustrating encoun-

ters and the final vision of the major himself being ridden through town not in pomp and circumstance but in tar and feathers. If Alger's stories are a kind of fairy tale, illuminating the Protestant ethic with an Alladin's lamp, then Hawthorne's is a tale of terror, wherein the light is supplied by the frightful gleam of torches.

Moreover, if we go all the way back to Poor Richard, we will find a somewhat different version of things from that promulgated in *Ragged Dick*, discovering that in Alger's version Franklin's persona is stuffed full of Longfellow's transcendental "Excelsior!" " 'God helps them that help themselves,' Poor Richard says in his Almanac of 1733," says Father Abraham in *The Way to Wealth*—only Poor Richard said it in 1736. In 1733, what Poor Richard said was "The favor of the great is no inheritance," thereby in his first almanac establishing a skeptical tone that endures throughout. When he framed his quietus in 1758, he surrounded his Father Abraham with an audience of unheeding fools, and the old man himself is something of a Polonius, his wisdom a catchphrase catechism of berries carefully picked out of brambles. Franklin is generally regarded as the apostle of the Protestant ethic, his *Autobiography* as a secular equivalent to the *Acts* of Saint Paul, but the man who wrote "Pride breakfasted with Plenty, dined with Poverty, supped with Infamy" ate at Shakespeare's table six days a week and fasted on the seventh.

"To be proud of Knowledge is to be blind with Light," wrote Poor Richard, paraphrasing eyeless Gloucester, and with Hamlet he observed that "Famine, plague, war, and an unnumbered throng of guilt-avenging ills, to man belongs." As for opportunity, it is "a great bawd," and though Poor Richard wrote "Innocence is its own defence," he also noted the less-often quoted "Distrust and Caution are the parents of Security." Still, Franklin's best-remembered invention is not Poor Richard but Honest Ben, and it was his *Autobiography* that provided Alger his fabulous formula; but in that book also we can detect a dark dimension, not a fall but a cynical shadow cast by the hero's passage upward. Moreover, if we range even further back in American time, to Franklin's own literary model, Cotton Mather's *Life of Sir William Phips*, and forward to a later version of the same genre, the *Narrative of the Life of Frederick Douglass, An American Slave*, we shall find a dark vein running through the golden flesh of the American Dream. A literary version of infected femoral artery, it points like a fiery red arrow to the clay foot of the climber, revealing the essential disjunctiveness of the American myth of success, the tragic dimension imperfectly concealed beneath the comic veneer. "You can't pray a lie," says ragged Huck, Mark Twain's response to Alger's myth, but the sad facts tell us that the author did otherwise, that *Huckleberry Finn* is no less a fiction than *Ragged Dick*. In America, living a lie is a way of life, as we shall see, wherein history as "his story" is, in the words of one who knew whereof he spoke, mostly "bunk."

2.

Ben Franklin, by his own account, is an American version of Dick Whittington, arriving in Philadelphia without a cat but with the same ability to land on his feet. As such, he is a preview of the Alger hero, and though hardly born poor, young Ben the printer's boy certainly suffered youthful adversity, attending the school of hard knocks administered by his older half-brother. In typical Alger fashion, Ben leaves home for New York City, and though he ended up in Philadelphia, the town where Alger sends his bad boys to mend their ways, it was a good enough Manhattan for Ben. Franklin's game is Alger's solitary sport, moreover, for by dint of hard work, regular habits, and, most important, a reputation for honesty, young Ben comes to the notice of a benefactor, no less than the governor of the province, Sir William Keith. "He said," writes Franklin, that "I appeared [to be] a young man of promising parts and therefore should be encouraged. The printers at Philadelphia were wretched ones, and if I would set up there, he made no doubt I should succeed; for his part, he would procure me the public business, and do me every other service in his power" (Max Farrand edition of the *Autobiography*).

Swollen with expectation, but in need of money to set up his print shop, Ben returned home to Boston bearing a letter from the governor to his father. In typical Alger fashion, he was "better dressed than ever . . . having a genteel new suit from head to foot, a watch, and my pockets lined with near five pounds sterling in silver." That timepiece is the most important article of furniture, not only as a symbol of Franklin's adage concerning the monetary value of minutes, but as a golden link in the Alger connection. For in Alger's stories the pocket watch has the same phallic power as the six-shooter west of the Mississippi, and when the successful Alger hero returns home, it is invariably with a Tiffany watch in his pocket, the Colt .45 of chronometers, the display of which sends the snobbish son of the town squire slinking off the stage with his gaudy Waterbury. So also with Ben and his older brother, who is "glum and sullen" when the prosperous young Philadelphian "took an opportunity of letting [him] see my watch," and who complained to his mother that Ben "had insulted him in such a manner . . . that he could never forget or forgive it."

In this, adds Franklin, "he was mistaken," but so was young Ben concerning financial help from his father, who thought he was too young for the responsibility. When Ben returned to Philadelphia with this sad news, Governor Keith offered to set him up in business and suggested that he travel to England to buy the necessary equipment, promising him "letters commendary to a number of his friends, besides [a] letter of credit, to furnish me with the necessary money for purchasing the press, types, paper, etc." But the letters were never forthcoming, and Ben was forced to sail without them, and in London he discovered the true character of his benefactor, for a friend assured him "there was not the least probability that he had written any letters for me, that no one who knew him had the smallest dependence on him, and he laughed at the idea of the Governor's giving me a letter of credit, having, as he said, no credit to give. On my expressing some concern about what I should do, he advised me to endeavor getting some employment in the way of my business. 'Among the printers here,' says he, 'you will improve yourself; and when you return to America, you will set up to greater advantage.' "

Which moral brings us back once again to Hawthorne's fable, not Alger's, for in Franklin's version of success there is no fairy godfather, no benevolent patron, no miraculous lift upwards, no break. Though the recipient of many little favors from other men, and by his own account a lucky man, Franklin is careful to stress throughout his autobiography that success is a sequence of small chances well seized—not an elevator but the rungs on a ladder. Ben Franklin, that is, is no sunburst of Enlightenment optimism but a careful, candlestick Prometheus for whom a faith in human nature was never so strong as his Calvinist conviction of universal depravity. After all, the Puritan genre on which he modeled his life story was the spiritual autobiography, the underlying principle of which is that of many only a few are chosen, and those by the arbitrary will of God. Franklin acknowledges the role of Providence in his rise, and therein lies the covenantal loophole, suggesting that it is a mistake to regard Franklin's *Autobiography* as a democratic parable. Addressing his book as an epistle to his bastard son, William Temple Franklin, the author provides an apologia for presuming to write an account of his own life: "From the poverty and obscurity in which I was born and in which I passed my earliest years, I have raised myself to a state of affluence and some degree of celebrity in the world. As constant good fortune has accompanied me even to an advanced period of life, my posterity will perhaps be desirous of learning the means, which I employed, and which, thanks to Providence, so well succeeded with me. They may also deem them fit to be imitated, should any of them find themselves in similar circumstances." In that last sentence lies the contractual small print.

The analogue to Franklin's *Autobiography* is Chesterfield's letters to *his* illegitimate son, not only in intention but effect, for both young men were notable failures at emulating their sires, a paradox that demonstrates the essential disjunctiveness of both books. Exemplary men, in two very different areas of Anglo-

American society, neither Franklin nor Chesterfield could be called common men; but whereas Chesterfield could at least endow his son with hereditary rank, the best Franklin could do for his boy was the governorship of New Jersey. If, as Poor Richard put it, "Half the Truth is often a great Lie," then Franklin's *Autobiography* is something of a fiction, at least as a formula for success. Franklin may promote himself as the eighteenth-century ideal, the *vir bonum*, but that ideal in the eighteenth century appears more often than not as a satiric exemplum, like Pope's Man of Ross a rara avis as well, surrounded by a cast of knaves and fools. So Franklin provides us with a statistical proof of his own sanctity, defining his success by the failures of others. His bullying half-brother, James, his fellow belletrist, Ralph, and his rival Philadelphia printer, Keimer, all provide young Ben a flattering backdrop, and they are but three from a cast of deceiving and self-deceiving characters whose deficiencies serve as aesthetic and often comic relief to his steady rise in life.

It must be said that Alger took this page also from Franklin's life, for tricky tradesmen were Alger's trick in trade, reminding us that a Unitarian is only a Presbyterian writ sideways. But there remains that strategic difference, the benevolent patron; and there is yet another disparity, for while Alger's boys were legion, there was only one Ben Franklin. There was, moreover, more self-interest and chicanery in Franklin's public dealings than he allows, but we forgive him his petty sins in acknowledging his great gifts, including that peculiar state of grace known as irony. Such was the pervasiveness of his wit that were we to point out to him his clay foot he would demonstrate its advantages in extinguishing small fires. Franklin puts himself forth as an example of what a new country can do for a poor boy from another city, but we return his wink, with the awareness that he was a very special case. Like so many of his jokes, the *Autobiography* depends for its effect on the implicit silence and the brevity that attend the exercise of wit, humor irradiating the space left by that which was not said. Franklin may not, in his *Autobiography*, have accommodated a tragic sense of life, but his comedy is that transcendent kind, by means of which the stolid shape of the hero casts an antic shadow that claps its hands and sings.

3.

Quite another shadow is cast by Sir William Phips, the hero of Cotton Mather's *Pietas in Patriam*, and the likeliest candidate for the honor of being America's first self-made man. Born on the Kennebeck River in the Province of Maine, in 1650, on the frontier of New England, Phips was the youngest of twenty-six children, a distinction guaranteed by the death of his father soon thereafter. Young Phips helped for a while on the family farm, herding sheep; but seeking to better himself, he turned to ship carpentry, and, then, ambitious to rise in the world, went up to Boston. There he first learned to read and write and next married a well-placed, though not wealthy, widow. Then, from building ships, Phips turned to sailing them. Hearing sailors' stories of a treasure hulk sunk off the Bahamas, Captain Phips sailed for England to obtain the necessary backing for the recovery of the gold, and after overcoming numerous obstacles, he finally made his lucky strike off the coast of Hispaniola, Haiti. Though the crown and Phips's backers got the lion's share of his Spanish gold, the Yankee skipper received a small fortune and, by way of consolation prize, a knighthood, and it was as Sir William that he sailed in triumph back to Boston.

   Though plainly a member of the elect, Sir William had unaccountably neglected to join the Congregational church, but he soon made up for that singular deficiency by applying to Increase Mather & Son, whose fortunes were henceforth identified with his own. After the Glorious Revolution, Phips celebrated the ascension of William and Mary by sailing off to Nova Scotia to capture Port Royal, and when he returned once again to Boston, he found that he had been made a magistrate of the colony. Not content with his triumphs, he mounted a campaign for the invasion of Canada, sailing up the Saint Lawrence in a fleet that was defeated by a combination of bad weather and superior French forces, a reversal of Phips's personal fortunes that plunged Massachusetts into a depression. As a dubious consolation prize, Phips was handed the governorship of that colony by Increase Mather, who had demanded that right as part of a package deal involving the new charter he had obtained from the king. Since the charter was less generous to the rest of Massachusetts, Mather's package added further weight to Phips's declining fortunes, and having received the highest office to which a poor boy from Maine could aspire, he began a steady descent.

To Governor Phips's credit was his use of his office to halt the witchcraft trials, but he did that only after his wife had been accused, and in other matters he proved a less than ideal choice for an office requiring tact and statesmanship. The very qualities that made for success on the high seas undid him in high places, and while allowing himself to be an instrument of the Mathers when it came to levying unpopular taxes to support the Church, Phips was very much his own man where free trade was the issue. He not only abused his authority by impeding the collection of customs duties, but accelerated the free exchange of goods by playing at pirate. Whatever he did, moreover, Phips did with a sailor's strong hand: confusing opposition with mutiny, he crushed his opponents instead of compromising with them, and even resorted to physical violence in his handling of customs officers who presumed to do their duty. As a result, four years after he was given the governorship, Phips was recalled to England to face charges of misconduct, but before he could be brought to trial, he had the good grace to die. Into the grave with him, pinned to his coffin like the funeral ode that Cotton Mather wrote for the occasion, went the political ambitions of Increase and his son.

Ponder, if you will, the mythic aspects of Phips's life: like Davy Crockett, William Henry Harrison, and Abe Lincoln, he was born on the frontier, a poor and self-educated boy; like Ben Franklin he went to the city and (after an adventuresome interval) found God; like George Washington he led an American army against the French and Indians; like Lee he suffered a crushing defeat; like Grant he was stained with corruption; like Hoover he presided over a depression that he in large part caused; like Eisenhower he ended a witch hunt by fiat when it got out of hand; and he narrowly escaped impeachment by dying, like Harding. Big with the mystical matter of American politics, Phips in terms of literature can be seen as a Marlovian hero, whose rise to power is flawed by a fatal hubris, an overreaching for further laurels and fame that tumbles him into defeat, a fall in fortune, and death—ignominy the last act of which was played out on the scene of his first triumph. One could read his story as a tragedy, that is to say, but Cotton Mather did not.

Instead, the foremost Puritan eulogist, who was styled by a contemporary poet as an "embalmer of the dead," undertook to erect a literary statue to the memory of Sir William by not only removing his warts but by performing drastic cosmetic surgery as well. Something in the nature of a posthumous campaign biography, his life of Phips creates a hero for the American strand, a Massachusetts Aeneas, *Phippius Maximus*, a champion of the Commonwealth whose motto is *Pietas in Patriam*, devoted love of country. Long before Weems's Washington cut down the cherry tree and confessed the truth in an immortal fiction, Parson Mather perfect the great American art of telling a lie for the sake of a higher verity. His immediate aim was as parochial as any sermon he wrote, still another attempt to recoup the Mathers' political fortunes; but the ultimate effect was transcendent, for the result of his effort is the shaping of the primal American action, the Protestant epic.

Mather's method throughout is to dignify his subject with great historical and classical analogies, in his opening chapter borrowing a page from Plutarch by comparing Phips's lowly origins with noble or heroic precedents and ending with Francisco Pizarro, the conqueror of Peru. These models are irradiated with a Puritan glory by endowing young Phips with "an unaccountable *impulse* upon his mind, persuading him . . . 'that he was born to greater matters.' " To anyone familiar with the language of Puritan election, that impulse is the litmus stain of innate nobility, the royal purple indicating the workings of grace within. A similar impulse carried Franklin out of Boston, his voyage signifying a divine right of passage upwards, and Phips likewise heads for town and from thence launches his Jason-like expedition. He sailed, notes Mather, in such a ship as that "which the Dutchmen stamped on their first coin, with these words about it: *Incertum quo Fata ferant*," a pagan motto with Providential implications. This is the first but hardly the last association Mather makes between his hero and currency, including the first floating of public credit in America. By such means he suggests that the flow of money is a fated matter, directed by a supernatural agency, a transcendent bureau of the Treasury which insures that the world's wealth ends up in the stewardship of certified Protestant accountants. Phips, plainly, is a hero of credit capital. Having, in Mather's terms, a *"capacity for business* in many considerable actions," he is a man for all business, which is to say a businessman, prototypal hero for the rising generation.

During his quest for the Spanish treasure, Mather's Phips evinced an "invincible," even "indefatigable *patience*," which, coupled with a "proportionable *diligence*," resulted in the overcoming of all "difficulties that had been thrown in his way." Though not heroic on the classical plan, these qualities are virtues emulated both by Ben Franklin and Alger's boys, and for Mather, likewise, the greatest prize obtained by his hero is not his title and his fortune but "the character of an *honest man*." Phips may be an American Jason, *"a knight of the golden fleece,"* but he is also " 'the knight of honesty,' for it was *honesty* with *industry* that raised him; and he became a mighty river, without the running in of muddy water to make him so. Reader, now make a pause, and behold *one raised by God*." As a shepherd raised to great place, as Mather's candidate for saintly patron of New England, Sir William Phips is cast in the shape of the great Biblical governor, David, the *"advanced shepherd,"* on whose coins were stamped "his old pouch and crook, the instrument of shepherdy," on one side, and on the other, "the towers of Zion." And because of his great success in fishing up gold for his king, Sir William is celebrated by Mather as a *"King's-fisher,"* with the suggestion that New England enjoyed *"halcyon* days" under his administration. But a kingfisher is not a fisher king, nor was Governor Phips exactly a scion of Prince Hal, having too much of Falstaff in his makeup. And as for David, who restored Jerusalem to the Jews, Phips did nothing of the sort, nor was he in his Canadian campaign a purely Christian hero, leading a holy war against the infidels of the North; for though Mather compares him to Caesar invading Britain, the purpose of Phips's adventure was plunder, not a *pax Puritanum*.

Mather does his best to make a guardian angel out of his unwieldy subject, who is dropped "as it were from the *machine of heaven*" to relieve "the distresses of the land," but one can detect the theatrical creaking of the gears in Mather's backstage engine. There are, that is to say, the detectable outlines of a sow's ear in Mather's silken portrait of Puritan virtue, a disjunctive dimension that promotes an unintentionally mock-heroic tone. "For his *exterior*," writes Mather of Phips's physical appearance, "he was one *tall*, beyond the common set of men, and *thick* as well as *tall*, and *strong* as well as *thick*: he was, in all respects, exceedingly *robust*, and able to conquer such difficulties of *diet* and of *travel*, as would have killed most men alive: nor did the *fat*, whereinto he grew very much in his later years, take away the vigor of his motions." Had Jonathan Swift written these lines, we would have called them exquisitely ironic, but Mather, alas, is deadly serious. Similar is Mather's description of Phips's "enterprising genius," a "disposition for business" that "was of the Dutch mold, where, with a little show of *wit* there is much *wisdom* demonstrated." But cheese is also cast in a Dutch mold, the bigness of which suggests anything but heroic proportions; and Mather describes his champion's chief talent as the ability to "prudently contrive a weighty undertaking, and then patiently pursue it unto the end. He was of an inclination cutting rather like a *hatchet* than like a *razor*; he would propose very considerable matters to himself, and then so cut *through* them, that no difficulties could be put by the *edge* of his resolution." Phips may have been, in Mather's phrase, of the "temper for doing great things," but a hatchet is hardly the heroic sword; nor are prudence and patience pagan virtues, but patently Puritan, being the kind of middle-class values for which the sons of New England were praised and the daughters named.

There is, therefore, a detectable stammer in Mather's attempt to convert by a twist of the tongue his favorite governor into a New England David, an unintended quality of burlesque in which the intended portrait progressively degenerates into caricature, much like the metamorphosis of Daumier's Louis Philippe into a vegetable. And these skips of the tongue carry us to the brink of a very chasm of credibility, the depths of which reveal an essential darkness at the core of Mather's hero, a disjunctiveness of metaphysical proportions. For in his account of General Phips's Canadian campaign, "the greatest action that ever the New Englanders attempted," Mather relates by way of analogue a rabbinical anecdote, concerning the "time when the Philistines had made some inroads and assaults from the northward upon the skirts of Goshen, where the Israelites had a residence, before their coming out of Egypt."

> The Israelites, and especially that active colony of the Ephraimites, were willing to revenge these injuries upon their wicked neighbors; they presumed themselves powerful and numerous enough to encounter the Canaanites, even in their own country; and they formed a brisk expedition, but came off unhappy losers in it. . . . The *time* was not yet come; there was more *haste* than good *speed* in the attempt; they were not enough concerned for the counsel and presence of God in the undertaking; they mainly propounded the *plunder* to be got among a people whose trade was that wherewith beasts enriched them; so the business miscarried. This history the Psalmist going to recite says, "I will utter dark sayings of old."

If Sir William is Mather's version of Spenser's knight, a militant saint but without a red cross, a *georgos* for the American strand, then in this parable lies his own dark conceit. The parallels between historical anecdote and the miscarried conquest of the Canadian Canaan are absolute, even to the allusion to the fur trade; yet Mather, who had the nose of a mole for "dark matters," refrains from exploring the analogy, ending instead by quoting his Boston kingfish, Sir William, who "would say, 'That the things which had befallen him in this expedition were too deep to be *dived* into!' "

Mather's unusual silence in this regard is part and parcel of his eulogizing portrait of Sir William, the holding of his tongue concerning the Canadian campaign resulting in one more instance of impeded speech. A Puritan author less concerned with apologetics, less involved personally with the fortunes of Governor Phips, would have used the failed invasion as the basis for a thundering jeremiad against the worship of false gods, but Mather does his best to plaster and paint over the imperfections of his carpenter saint. Threfore, if Phips's greatest fault was overweening ambition, a wolfish hunger for power and recognition draped by Mather with the sheepskin of "*humility* and *lowliness*," then the author's own besetting sin was that which the Puritans most abhorred—Hypocrisy, that creature which so often in allegory rides attendance on Pride. The *Magnalia* is often read (or at least talked about) as a massive jeremiad, an epical castigation of the rising generation by means of a celebration of the original Puritan errand, but the implications of Mather's life of Phips, which (like the life of David in the Bible) is the longest biography in his book, suggests otherwise. In raising his "statue" (as he put it) of his New World hero, Mather in effect places it atop a cenotaph of the dead hopes of the first generation, the transcendent errand of converting Indians to Christianity having become the imperial mission of eradicating them from the land, the hope of planting a millenial light in the New World transformed into the crushing of the Canadian Carthage. In 1623 Edward Winslow prophesied that profit and piety would "jump together" in America, but in the great potato-sack race that ensued, the profit motive increasingly provided the foot power; and if Phips as a hero and the *Magnalia* as an epic are flawed, it is a disjunctiveness that extends to the very base rock of the Puritan errand, split asunder by the schism between their mercantile and missionary purposes.

Ben Franklin, as self-cast hero, contains a similar crack, much like the one in the Liberty Bell, a deep division between the promise of New World opportunity and the reality, between Enlightenment optimism and a Whiggish faith in progress and Calvinist gloom supported by a Tory faith in mechanisms of stability, like the regulating agencies that Franklin established in the City of Brotherly Love, placing a lamp on every street corner and a policeman under every lamp. This same division is contained in the disparity between the Declaration of Independence and the Constitution, one declaring self-evident truths concerning the rights of individuals, the other setting up mechanisms by means of which those rights are kept in check, lest they develop into tyranny, whether of presidents or the proletariat. The Declaration is a manifesto, a millennial proclamation, the Constitution a body of laws founded on the sacredness of property, both thereby evincing a disjunctiveness similar to that of the Puritan utopia, where the Cambridge Platform belied the democratic principles of Congregationalism by elevating a theocratic elite, those saints who were more saintly than the rest. The Platform casts a long shadow, moreover, becoming the kind of scaffold from which men were sold to other men, a transaction protected by the shibboleth of property even as it belied the proposition concerning the equality of *all* men, under God, Amen.

4.

That shadow in time became a towering Babylon of prosperity, a blackness of the kind Cotton Mather preferred not to peer into, inhabited by a people whose transplantation to America was in all ways different from the Puritan exodus, but a people whose identity is inescapably linked to a prayerful captivity on the banks of many a southern Euphrates, whence they looked north toward a distant Canaan with infinite longing. There is no more telling account of the anguish of being black in nineteenth-century America than Frederick Douglass' account of his life in bondage, an agonizing parable of the meaning of success to a man whose skin is not white. In many ways, the black man in America is the white man's shadow, and Douglass is Ben Franklin's specific shade, his book assuming the shape of a spiritual autobiography also. But Douglass' is definably a *black* book, in Gothic characters, putting forth the outlines of the Protestant epic in reverse, being not a record of essays to do good but attempts to be bad,

Douglass like Milton's Satan inventing virtue from an evil necessity. But if Douglass' narrative is a perversion of the Protestant epic, a demonstration of a massively disjunctive element in American life, it also manifests *its* essential flaw, an ontological fault in the little, lower layer, the *corium*, which is neither white or black, but red, signifying our universal mortality.

Like Ben Franklin, Douglass identified his rise in life with a trip to the city, in his case the scene of Agnew's ascension, Baltimore. Removed while still a child from the brutalizing life on a Chesapeake Bay plantation, young Douglass (or Bailey as he was then called) was sent to a Baltimore household where he was to be servant to a white boy. Douglass declared:

> Going to live at Baltimore laid the foundation, and opened the gateway to all my subsequent prosperity. I have ever regarded it as the first plain manifestation of that kind providence which has ever since attended me, and marked my life with so many favors. I regarded the selection of myself as being somewhat remarkable. There were a number of slave children that might have been sent from the plantation to Baltimore. There were those younger, those older, and those of the same age. I was chosen from among them all, and was the first, last, and only choice.

These are familiar, Franklinesque statistics, the numerical odds of the Protestant epic, but Douglass' version of spiritual autobiography takes its cast from the slave's identification with Israel in captivity, by means of which the Chesapeake is transformed from a Euphrates to a River Jordan, a symbol of passage to a better world: "I placed myself in the bows of the sloop," he recalls, "and there spent the remainder of the day in looking ahead, interesting myself in what was in the distance rather than in things near by or behind."

One of the most remarkable passages in Douglass' narrative is his Byronic apostrophe to the bay, "whose broad bosom was ever white with sails from every quarter of the habitable globe," ships whose unimpeded movements and immaculate whiteness were mocking symbols of freedom to the chained black man, holding out both the hope, and hopefully the means, of escape. "It cannot be," young Bailey reasons, "that I shall live and die a slave. I will take to the water. This very bay shall yet bear me into freedom. . . . There is a better day coming." Though Baltimore proved a blessing, it was but a greater Babylon, haunted by the curse of bondage, and though Douglass, like William Phips, learned to read and write in the city, he realized likewise that his destiny lay elsewhere. Yet Baltimore was the scene of a sort of epiphany for Douglass, for it was there he learned the terrible truth of the black man's ignorance: "It was a new and special revelation, explaining dark and mysterious things, with which my youthful understanding had struggled, but struggled in vain. I now understood what had been to me a most perplexing difficulty—to wit, the white man's power to enslave the black man. It was a grand achievement, and I prized it highly." Realizing that only so long as he was kept in darkness could a black man be kept in bondage, Douglass henceforth redoubled his efforts to educate himself, a struggle toward the light which pitted his will for the first time against that of his white master. Though it was his master's wife who first taught the young black boy his ABCs, his master's opposition to further instruction proved equally instrumental, since it was the white man's fear of the black man's awakening from ignorance that convinced Douglass of the power of knowledge. "In learning to read," he testifies, "I owe almost as much to the bitter opposition of my master, as to the kindly aid of my mistress. I acknowledge the benefit of both."

This paradox of blessed antagonism is a version of the role that adversity plays in the scheme of the Protestant epic, the proper use of enemies in getting ahead. Without making the parallel explicit, moreover, Douglass in effect casts himself as a black Adam, his learning to read being a version of the Fortunate Fall, and despite his conventional piety, he casts his white master as an angry and punishing deity, but a God who resembles Satan more than Jehovah. Douglass throughout his narrative plays upon the many bitter paradoxes engendered by the slave system, a world in which truth is punished and a lie rewarded, but none is more strategic than the situation that emerges between the black man and the white over the matter of Douglass' education:

> Though conscious of the difficulty in learning without a teacher, I set out with high hope, and a fixed purpose, at whatever cost of trouble, to learn how to read. The very decided manner with which [my master] spoke, and strove to impress his wife with the evil consequences of giving me instruction, served to convince me that he was deeply sensible of the truths he was uttering. It gave me the best assurance that I might rely with the utmost confidence on the results which, he said, would flow from teaching me to read. What he most dreaded, that I most desired. What he most loved, that I most hated. That which to him was a great evil, to be carefully shunned, was to me a great good, to be diligently sought; and the argument which he so warmly urged, against my learning to read, only served to inspire me with a desire and determination to learn.

A black Faust, an enchained Prometheus stealing white fire, Douglass by means of his ironic reversals transforms the world of slavery into that deepest South of all, a place where the reigning deity calls Evil his Good, and where the most religious white men are the most demonic persecutors of their helpless slaves. In the land of Mary, Christ not the Devil wears a black skin. Still, the greatest paradox is that Douglass is inspired to escape his hell by means of the white man's instrument, the book, a regnant symbol also in Franklin's account of how he corrected his youthful errata. Douglass early points out that the black man's sole means of self-expression is song, that black "culture" is solely an expression of misery, a long, black psalm by means of which the slave may find relief through lament. But as an expression of hopelessness the black man's song is a passive instrument, and for Douglass power comes from between the covers of a book. His is a dialectic of revolution not unlike Mao's, for it is by means of such implements of the white man's world as the *Columbian Orator*, a manual of rhetoric expressing republican ideals, that Douglass makes his arduous and by no means uninterrupted flight from bondage to freedom, using his enemy's own weapons to defeat him.

Along the way, Douglass learns also the meaning of black brotherhood, and yet, when the opportunity to escape presents itself, he does leave his brothers behind him. Still, Douglass soon enlisted in the abolition movement, a decision the account of which occupies a small but important place in his *Narrative*, a disjunctive element depending upon an earlier episode for its meaning. During his last years in slavery, Douglass worked as a ship caulker in Baltimore, learning a trade that increased his self-reliance and provided the money facilitating his escape. But in this as in all things, the aspiring young black ran into a wall of whiteness, sharing the abuse heaped on free "colored" workmen by white carpenters who feared "that if free colored carpenters were encouraged, they would soon take the trade into their own hands, and poor white men would be thrown out of employment." The tension, as so often happens in Douglass' narrative, erupted in violence, of which he was the victim, being turned upon by the boy-apprentices with whom he worked, a beating cheered by the older white men: "Such was, and such remains," observes Douglass bitterly, "the state of things in the Christian city of Baltimore."

Contrast to Baltimore is provided by New Bedford, where everything is "clean, new, and beautiful," where men work cheerfully and with dignity, surrounded by "splendid churches, beautiful dwellings, and finely-cultivated gardens; evincing an amount of wealth, comfort, taste, and refinement, such as I had never seen in any part of slaveholding Maryland." Douglass' New Bedford, like Mather's Boston, is something of a new Jerusalem; yet when the now-free black man, anticipating with "rapture" the joys of being his "own master," seeks work, "the reward of which was to be entirely my own," he discovers that New Bedford is but old Baltimore down at the docks: "I went in pursuit of a job of calking; but such was the strength of prejudice against color, among the white calkers, that they refused to work with me, and of course I could get no employment." With a shrug, Douglass "threw off my calking habiliments, and prepared myself to do any kind of work I could get to do . . . no work too hard—none too dirty," a life at hard labor from which he was soon rescued by the abolition movement. Douglass does not dwell on the prejudice he encountered in New Bedford, for it was not to the point of his narrative, but it is much to the point of the argument here. With Franklin and Mather, Douglass was writing revisionist biography, and with a certain audience and effect in mind. It would not do, in 1845, to point out to northern whites their failings, for it was in their hands that the fate of the black man lay. The cause of abolition therefore was best served by flattery, by drawing neat distinctions between benighted Maryland and enlightened Massachusetts.

For similar reasons, Douglass glosses over another element of disjunctiveness provided by his fellow blacks, for in celebrating the brotherhood of slaves, he neglects to note that one of his earlier attempts to escape was betrayed by one of his own. This is not to diminish either the man or his cause, but merely to point out that Douglass, like Franklin, was a pragmatic realist. Much more important, moreover, is the implicit demonstration by Douglass' subsequent experience in America that the paradox of white and black continues north of the Mason-Dixon Line, in the society of crusaders as well as carpenters. For Douglass attained the kind of worldly prominence that distinguishes the rising action of the Protestant epic only by abandoning the world of work and wage for that very special arena of radical reform. As at the very beginning he was chosen from many for salvation in Baltimore, so in New Bedford he succeeded finally as a special case, indeed as a case in point, licensing his use as a walking, talking symbol to the abolition movement, in whose service his narrative was written, as proof that such an effective orator had indeed been a slave. Douglass became, that is to say, a personification of the book that taught him the meaning of freedom, a Columbian orator; but in doing so he made manifest that self-evident truth about being black in America, that blackness assumes the shape of the white man's shadow. In casting off his former identity, the young escaped slave turned to his white benefactor in New Bedford, Nathan Johnson, and asked him for a new name. Since, as he tells us, "Mr. Johnson had just been reading the 'Lady of the Lake,' [he] at once suggested that my name be 'Douglass.' " What he does not tell us is that the name of the legendary Scots highlander means "the black one," that in this uniquely literary baptism at "the starting point of a new existence," the white man Johnson gave the black man Bailey a symbolic identity indeed; and Douglass' subsequent role in agitating for abolition suggests that Mark Twain wrote more truly than he realized when he said that Sir Walter Scott was responsible for the Civil War.

In sum, Frederick Douglass' narrative, like Ben Franklin's, is a tale of two cities, and if Douglass found truth in Baltimore, he discovered the essential lie of New Bedford, a lie he was willing to ignore for the sake of his brothers still languishing in Babylon. Indeed, his subsequent career as a public speaker was mounted from a scaffolding that, like the Cambridge Platform, was planted in the unsure ground of an essential fallacy, a career that ironically was dependent on the continued plight of the black man. Following the Union victory, Douglass worked for a time in Reconstruction, but his career ended with a series of government sinecures, rewards certainly earned by his public services but which held out no real hope of attainment to his fellow black freedmen. Thus the secret burden of Douglass' book is the theme of *Native Son*, that America North and South remains white territory—that the black man can enjoy freedom only if he escapes into the elusive shadow of his own identity. In the company of white men, as on the television screen, he is often filtered into a perfect black blank, Ellison's invisible man. But among his own, assuming the shape of perpetual rebellion against the white man's world, he can find in pride the only response possible to prejudice, but a pride that is either the prelude to tragedy or the product of persecution, either a fatal hubris or a form of election, a state of grace dependent upon the singular proofs of suffering, either a Nat Turner or a Martin Luther King, a Spartacus or a Christ. Among Frederick Douglass' other services for the sake of his cause was to provide inspiration for Harriet Beecher Stowe's *Uncle Tom's Cabin*, where he appears not as the Christly Tom but as the Byronic rebel, George Harris, that manifestly white man suffering from the accident of a black skin.

5.

Douglass, in short, even in celebrating his escape from bondage to freedom evinces the dark dimension of the American Dream, the disjunctive division between the hope of so many and its realization by so few, thereby providing a black counterpart to the comedy of Ben Franklin. The disparity that is the reality of American life is a chasm over which Horatio Alger built a bridge, suspended from skyhooks of wish fulfillment, providing a shortcut to the Celestial City that is not on Bunyan's map, being a rainbow over the Valley of the Shadow of Death. Those who take that route risk a terrible fall, as with Sir William Phips discovering the truth of wisdom most ancient, that "Success has ruin'd many a Man." For, says Poor Richard, "You may give a man an Office, but you cannot give him Discretion." Poor Richard also warns that we are to "think of three things: whence you came, where you are going, and to whom you must account"—wisdom of the sort that made Jefferson tremble for his countrymen. "One man may be more cunning than another," says Poor Richard, "but not more cunning than every body else," calling to mind similar words attributed to another Father Abraham, and reminding us also of impoverished Richard Nixon. "Take this remark from Richard, poor and lame, / Whate'er is begun in anger, ends in shame," writes Franklin's Poor Dick, who also wrote "the Wise and the Brave dares own that he was wrong" and that "tricks and treachery are the practice of fools that have not wit enough to be honest."

One could go on, but enough is as good as a feast where aphorisms are concerned, half a word being sufficient for the wise, though we might add, with Poor Richard, that "pardoning the Bad, is injuring the Good." But the main point to be made here is that Richard Nixon is yet another demonstration of the disjunctiveness inherent in the American dream, being the kind of "good Example" which for Poor Richard is "the best Sermon," his rise and fall dramatizing once again the difference between the ideal of Franklin's *Autobiography* and the reality of Poor Richard's wisdom. For a time it seemed that Nixon's hospital bed would prove to be his tomb, the man his own monument of mortality, lying supine, his clay foot elevated and exposed for the world to see, an epical case of gout. But Nixon lives, and thereby occupies an Argentina of the mind, a middle zone, neither comic nor tragic but both, an absurd stage in a theater evoking not laughter or tears but a certain numbness at the core, a vacuum-packed center.

Still, as Phips had his rabbinical Mather, so Nixon had his Rabbi Korff, and certainly the outlines of Nixon's life approximate the plot of the Protestant epic, being something of a travesty on the version promulgated by Horatio Alger, a myth casting its own shadow of antimyth. Nixon worked long and hard, very long and very hard, to attain his final place of power and privilege, his ascension a twenty-year climb up the greased pole of American politics, and the godlike Eisenhower reached down a helpful hand at the critical moment. True, once Eisenhower discovered what he had hold of he tried to let go, but our hero clung to his advantage, and ended up on the old man's shoulders. "Let's win this one for Ike!" he cried as the general lay dying, and though Nixon fell, he rose again on the third election year thereafter, being, as he put it, an idea whose time had come, defeating a man who likewise demonstrated the Alger myth, indeed who carried Horatio's name in an alliterative series of his own. Well, Nixon's idea has now passed into memory, fading as fast as a bad dream, and as it retreats into our political past, it diminishes, allowing for a certain interpretive perspective. It is wrong, I think, to conceive of Nixon as another Sir William Phips, hungry for power and fame. In all that Nixon did, one great thought, one hope is made manifest, his attainment of the highest office in the land being merely a passage to that Canaan of the middle class, *retirement*, not only in California or Florida, but in both of those best possible worlds.

For what is retirement, after all, but a terrestrial version of the Protestant heaven, where saints may enjoy the exquisite pleasure of watching other men work while doing nothing at all. Sir William Phips, as Mather points out, *could* have retired after finding his treasure, but unfortunately he decided to "venture my life in doing of good," to "expose myself, while I am able, and as far as I am able, for the service of my country," being "born for others, as well as myself." Franklin, likewise, retired from business at forty-two, henceforth asking what to Poor Richard was the "noblest question in the world: *What good may I do in it?*" For with Lucan, as with Phips, Franklin believed that a man was born "not for himself, but for the whole world." And Frederick Douglass, also, retired from the abolitionist movement into the world of Reconstruction, agitating for the civil rights of freedmen, before he finally sailed off for a long-deserved rest in Haiti, off the coast of which Sir William found his gold. But as Richard Nixon used the power of the presidency to promote world peace, so he turned the perquisites of his office into a guarantee of his own future tranquility, feathering such nests as only California can provide, a nest turned into a bed of thorns. For there are, according to Poor Richard, "no handsome prisons," and his namesake has enjoyed a most dubious felicity at San Clemente, exemplifying the wisdom that "Severity is often Clemency; Clemency, Severity."

As for the rest of us, we may thank our stars that Franklin presided in fact as well as spirit over the Constitutional Convention. For not only was the wisdom of Poor Richard accommodated by a governing mechanism designed to subvert the machinations of such as Richard M. Nixon, but Franklin was on the committee that framed the clause concerning impeachment, offering as his opinion that there were two ways of handling malfeasance in high office, and that the other way was political assassination. It was Franklin, you will recall, who also suggested the turkey instead of the eagle for our national emblem, the turkey being at least an honest bird, and bearing in mind Richard M. Nixon's favorite, spread-eagle cruciform pose, let us end with the last aphorism from Poor Richard's last almanac: "Rob not God, nor the Poor, lest thou ruin thyself; The Eagle snatched a Coal from the Altar, but it fired her Nest."

Notes on
Contributors

CLARENCE GOHDES, James B. Duke Professor of English Emeritus at Duke University, is the author of *The Periodicals of American Transcendentalism* (1931), *American Literature in Nineteenth-Century England* (1944), *Literature and Theater of the States and Regions of the U.S.A.: An Historical Bibliography* (1967), and *Bibliographical Guide to the Study of the Literature of the U.S.A.* (1970). He has edited *Uncollected Lectures of Ralph Waldo Emerson* (1933).

ARLIN TURNER was professor of English and editor of *American Literature* at Duke University. He was the author of *George W. Cable, a Biography* (1956), *Mark Twain and G. W. Cable: The Record of a Literary Friendship* (1960), *Nathaniel Hawthorne: An Introduction and Interpretation* (1961), and *Nathaniel Hawthorne: A Biography* (1980). He also edited *Hawthorne as Editor: Selections from His Writings in "The American Magazine for Useful and Entertaining Knowledge"* (1961).

WILLIAM L. ANDREWS is associate professor of English at the University of Wisconsin. He is coeditor of *Southern Literary Culture: 1969–1975* (1979) and the author of *The Literary Career of Charles W. Chesnutt* (1980). In 1976 he received the Norman Foerster Prize from the editors of *American Literature*.

LOUIS D. RUBIN, JR., is University Distinguished Professor of English at the University of North Carolina. Among his many books are *Thomas Wolfe: The Weather of His Youth* (1955);

The Faraway Country: Writers of the Modern South (1967),
George W. *Cable: The Life and Times of a Southern Heretic*
(1969), with Blyden Jackson, *Black Poetry in America: Two Essays in Historical Interpretation* (1974), *William Elliott Shoots a
Bear: Essays on the Southern Literary Imagination* (1976), and
The Wary Fugitives: Four Poets and the South (1978). He has
edited *The Curious Death of the Novel: Essays in American
Literature* (1967), *A Bibliographical Guide to the Study of South-
ern Literature* (1969), *The Comic Imagination in American Literature* (1973), with C. Hugh Holman, *Southern Literary Study:
Problems and Possibilities* (1975), with Robert Bain and Joseph
M. Flora, *Southern Writers: A Biographical Dictionary* (1979),
The Literary South (1979), and *The American South: Portrait of
a Culture* (1980).

C. HUGH HOLMAN is Kenan Professor of English at the Uni-
versity of North Carolina. Among his many books are *Thomas
Wolfe* (1960), *Three Modes of Modern Southern Fiction* (1966),
The Roots of Southern Writing (1972), *The Immoderate Past:
The Southern Writer and History* (1977), *Windows on the World:
Essays on American Social Fiction* (1979), and *A Handbook to
Literature* (4th ed., 1980). He has edited *The Short Novels of
Thomas Wolfe* (1961) and *Views and Reviews, by W. G. Simms*
(1962). He is coeditor with Louis D. Rubin of the *Southern
Literary Journal*.

PANTHEA REID BROUGHTON is professor of English at
Louisiana State University. She has written *William Faulkner:
The Abstract and the Actual* (1974) and has edited *The Art of
Walker Percy: Stratagems for Being* (1979).

JOHN SEELYE is Alumni Distinguished Professor of English at
the University of North Carolina. He is the author of *The True
Adventures of Huckleberry Finn* (1970), *Melville: The Ironic
Diagram* (1970), and *Prophetic Waters: The River in Early
American Life and Literature, 1582–1730* (1977), and *Mark
Twain in the Movies: A Meditation* (1977). He has written two
novels, *The Kid* (1972) and *Dirty Tricks* (1974).